Workbook

Entrepreneurship: Ideas in Action

SIXTH EDITION

Cynthia L. Greene

SOUTH-WESTERN
CENGAGE Learning

Australia • Brazil • Mexico • Singapore • United Kingdom • United States

For product information and technology assistance, contact us at **Cengage Learning Academic Resource Center, 1-800-423-0563**.

For permission to use material from this text or product, submit all requests online at **www.cengage.com/permissions**. Further permissions questions can be emailed to **permissionrequest@cengage.com**.

ISBN: 978-1-305-65310-8

Cengage Learning
20 Channel Center Street
Boston, MA 02210
USA

Cengage Learning is a leading provider of customized learning solutions with employees residing in nearly 40 different countries and sales in more than 125 countries around the world. Find your local representative at **www.cengage.com**.

Cengage Learning products are represented in Canada by Nelson Education, Ltd.

For your course and learning solutions, visit **ngl.cengage.com**.

Visit our company website at **www.cengage.com**.

Printed in the United States of America
Print Number: 01   Print Year: 2016

Contents

Chapter 8 Locate and Set Up Your Business

Chapter 9 Plan and Track Your Finances

Chapter 10 Operations Management

Chapter 11 Human Resource Management

Chapter 12 Risk Management

Chapter 13 Management for the Future

1.1 All About Entrepreneurship

True or False

Directions   Place a *T* for True or an *F* for False in the Answers column to show whether each of the following statements is true or false.

Answers

1. Entrepreneurs try to meet the needs of the marketplace by supplying a product or service.

   1._____

2. Entrepreneurs and employees are both directly affected by the consequences of the decisions they make.

   2._____

3. There are generally four types of businesses: manufacturing, wholesaling, retailing, and franchising.

   3._____

4. Entrepreneurial businesses include retailing businesses, such as clothing and furniture stores, but do not include service businesses.

   4._____

5. Manufacturing businesses produce the products they sell.

   5._____

6. A travel agency is a retailing business.

   6._____

7. Small businesses with fewer than 500 employees represent about 25 percent of all businesses in the United States today.

   7._____

8. Small businesses contribute billions of dollars to the U.S. economy every year.

   8._____

9. The failure rate for restaurants is higher than for other types of small businesses.

   9._____

10. The owner's business experience is a factor that contributes to the likelihood of success.

    10._____

Multiple Choice

Directions   In the Answers column, write the letter that represents the word, or group of words, that correctly completes the statement.

Answers

1. A person who takes the risk of a business venture is (a) not directly affected by the consequences of his or her decisions, (b) an employee, (c) an entrepreneur, (d) sure to be successful.

   1._____

2. A person who works for someone else is (a) an entrepreneur, (b) an employee, (c) the one who receives the profits of the business, (d) taking the risk of business venture.

   2._____

3. Manufacturing businesses (a) produce the products they sell, (b) sell products directly to the people who consume them, (c) sell services rather than products, (d) take resources out of the ground so that they can be consumed.

   3._____

4. Which of the following is a retailing business? (a) Automotive repair shop, (b) Travel agency, (c) Grocery store, (d) Farm.

   4._____

5. An entrepreneur who is green focuses on (a) helping others who are in need, (b) operating with integrity, (c) finding societal needs that are not being met by the government, (d) conserving resources.

   5._____

6. Since the end of the recession in 2009, small businesses have (a) decreased in number, (b) struggled more than large businesses, (c) generated the majority of new jobs, (d) contributed an average of $2 billion per year to the U.S. economy.

   6._____

7. About how many new businesses do *not* survive beyond five years? (a) About 10 percent, (b) Nearly one-quarter, (c) About half, (d) Almost 90 percent.

   7._____

8. Which of the following is a major factor in a small business's success? (a) Having adequate capital, (b) The owner's education level, (c) The owner's reason for starting the business, (d) All of these.

   8._____

Problem Solving

Directions   Answer the following questions in the space provided.

1. The first column of the following table lists what each of the six types of businesses does. Complete the table by identifying the type of business and providing three examples of the business.

	Type of Business	Examples
Sells products to other businesses rather than the final customer		
Sells services rather than products		
Generates fresh produce and other farm products		
Sells products directly to the people who use or consume them		
Takes resources out of the ground so that they can be consumed		
Produces the products it sells		

2. A consumer bought a pair of shoes at Heavenly Soles. The shoes were made by Sierra Shoes. Heavenly Soles purchased the shoes, which were part of a large shipment, from Hughes Apparel. Two years later, the consumer had the heels of the shoes repaired at Casey's Shoe Repair. Identify each of these businesses according to its type of entrepreneurial business.

Manufacturing business _____

Wholesaling business _____

Retailing business _____

Service business _____

1.2 Entrepreneurship and You

True or False

Directions Place a *T* for True or an *F* for False in the Answers column to show whether each of the following statements is true or false.

Answers

1. Successful entrepreneurs need to be self-confident because they must make decisions alone, but they do not need to be creative because they can hire creative people.

   1. _____

2. Being a good team member involves commitment, cooperation, and creativity.

   2. _____

3. Everyone has the qualities and aptitude needed to become a successful entrepreneur.

   3. _____

4. To determine if entrepreneurship is right for you, you need to perform a self-assessment.

   4. _____

5. Many entrepreneurs center a business on a hobby.

   5. _____

6. Aptitude is the ability to evaluate your strengths and weaknesses.

   6. _____

7. Entrepreneurship involves risk, which is both an advantage and a disadvantage.

   7. _____

8. An advantage of entrepreneurship is that nobody tells an entrepreneur what to do.

   8. _____

9. An advantage of entrepreneurship is that entrepreneurs make all decisions by themselves.

   9. _____

Multiple Choice

Directions   In the Answers column, write the letter that represents the word, or group of words, that correctly completes the statement.

Answers

1. Researchers have determined that successful entrepreneurs (a) want to make their own decisions, (b) do not always know what they want, (c) like to have someone else make decisions, (d) do not need to set goals.

   1. _____

2. Which of the following is *not* a characteristic of a successful entrepreneur? (a) Determination, (b) Creativity, (c) Dependence, (d) Self-confidence.

   2. _____

3. Competency involves (a) being able to look at things from different perspectives, (b) sharing ideas with others both verbally and in written form, (c) working well with others, (d) having the right set of skills needed to get the job done.

   3. _____

4. A self-assessment is an evaluation of your (a) hobbies and interests, (b) strengths and weaknesses, (c) past job experience, (d) ability to act quickly.

   4. _____

5. To determine your suitability for entrepreneurship, you should assess your (a) strengths and weaknesses, (b) interests, (c) aptitude, (d) all of these.

   5. _____

6. Two key factors that aid an entrepreneur's commitment to a business are (a) hobbies and sales experience, (b) interests and past experiences, (c) interests and sales experience, (d) hobbies and athletic ability.

   6. _____

7. Aptitude is the ability to (a) act quickly, (b) evaluate interests, (c) learn a particular kind of job, (d) all of these.

   7. _____

8. An advantage of entrepreneurship is that entrepreneurs (a) can supervise others, (b) make all decisions by themselves, (c) can work in a field that interests them, (d) do not need to set goals.

   8. _____

9. A disadvantage of entrepreneurship is that entrepreneurs (a) face irregular incomes, (b) must make all decisions by themselves, (c) work long hours, (d) all of these.

   9. _____

Problem Solving

Directions   In the space below, list eight characteristics of successful entrepreneurs. For each, explain how a lack of the characteristic could contribute to the failure of a business.

1. _____
   _____
   _____
   _____

2. _____
   _____
   _____
   _____

3. _____
   _____
   _____
   _____

4. _____
   _____
   _____
   _____

5. _____
   _____
   _____
   _____

6. _____
   _____
   _____
   _____

7. _____
   _____
   _____
   _____

8. _____
   _____
   _____
   _____

1.3 Explore Ideas and Opportunities

True or False

Directions   Place a *T* for True or an *F* for False in the Answers column to show whether each of the following statements is true or false.

Answers

1. An opportunity is a thought or concept that comes from creative thinking.

1._____

2. Analyzing past experiences and jobs is a good way to come up with a business idea.

2._____

3. You can learn about business opportunities by talking to other entrepreneurs.

3._____

4. Assessing different business opportunities helps you identify those that have the best chance for success.

4._____

5. It is not necessary to determine how much money it will take to start a business because you will be able to borrow the money that you need.

5._____

6. To decide whether or not a business opportunity is realistic for you, compare your background and experience with the experience of people who own that kind of business.

6._____

7. A SMART goal is specific, measurable, attainable, realistic, and timely.

7._____

8. Financial goals may include how quickly you can pay off your debts.

8._____

9. Nonfinancial goals are only for entrepreneurs who are solely interested in financial gain.

9._____

Multiple Choice

Directions   In the Answers column, write the letter that represents the word, or group of words, that correctly completes the statement.

Answers

1. Possibilities that arise from existing conditions are (a) ideas, (b) opportunities, (c) dreams, (d) goals.

1._____

2. People who excel at their jobs (a) have generally learned much about their profession, (b) see how successful marketing is conducted, (c) know how to satisfy customer needs, (d) all of these.

2._____

3. The Small Business Administration (SBA) (a) holds trade shows, (b) publishes information that may be helpful for small businesses, (c) has a department in most public libraries, (d) buys products from entrepreneurs to help them make a profit.

3._____

4. Special meetings where companies of the same industry or related industries display their products are (a) trade shows, (b) entrepreneurial conventions, (c) job fairs, (d) poor places to learn about opportunities.

4._____

5. All of the following can help you determine if a business opportunity is realistic *except* (a) the rate of business failure, (b) the market for that kind of business, (c) the background needed to run that kind of business, (d) the interest rates for loans at different banks.

5._____

6. When comparing different business opportunities, an entrepreneur should (a) set financial goals, (b) set nonfinancial goals, (c) determine the hours a week needed to run the business, (d) perform a self-assessment.

6._____

7. Financial goals can include (a) the best retirement age, (b) the monetary value of serving a community need, (c) how much money you will earn, (d) how many employees you will have in ten years.

7._____

8. Nonfinancial goals are important for an entrepreneur because they (a) determine personal satisfaction, (b) increase sales, (c) guarantee success, (d) enable a business to earn a profit.

8._____

Problem Solving

Directions   Answer the following questions in the space provided.

1. What is the difference between an opportunity and an idea?

   _____

   _____

   _____

   _____

   _____

2. List three places where you can go to find information about business opportunities.

   _____

   _____

   _____

   _____

   _____

3. For one of the places you listed in Question 2, describe the types of resources available.

   _____

   _____

   _____

   _____

   _____

4. How does comparing different business opportunities help you choose the one that will be the most successful for you?

   _____

   _____

   _____

   _____

   _____

5. Give three examples of a financial goal and three examples of a nonfinancial goal.

   _____

   _____

   _____

   _____

   _____

Name _____ Class _____ Date _____

1.4 Problem Solving for Entrepreneurs

True or False

Directions   Place a *T* for True or an *F* for False in the Answers column to show whether each of the following statements is true or false.

1. The best entrepreneurs use a formal problem-solving model to make decisions.   1. _____

2. Defining and quantifying the problem is the first step in the problem-solving model.   2. _____

3. Quantifying a problem helps a business owner determine how much it is worth to them to solve it.   3. _____

4. Identifying one or two possible solutions is usually sufficient.   4. _____

5. The problem-solving process is not complete until the action is evaluated.   5. _____

6. Good communication and listening skills are vital to the problem-solving process.   6. _____

7. Brainstorming is always done in a group setting; it is a useless activity for an individual.   7. _____

8. Following a brainstorming session, a decision should be made immediately.   8. _____

9. Entrepreneurs should not be afraid of making mistakes.   9. _____

Multiple Choice

Directions   In the Answers column, write the letter that represents the word, or group of words, that correctly completes the statement.

Answers

1. A formal problem-solving model (a) consists of five steps, (b) is never necessary for everyday decisions, (c) is used only to gather information, (d) helps people solve problems in a logical manner.   1. _____

2. Which of the following is *not* a step in the decision-making process? (a) Identify various solutions, (b) Take action, (c) Evaluate the problem, (d) Gather information.   2. _____

3. After the problem is defined and information gathered, you (a) try to quantify the problem, (b) identify various solutions, (c) make your decisions, (d) reach a consensus.   3. _____

4. In evaluating alternatives and selecting the best option, you (a) gather information about each alternative, (b) see if the selected alternative works, (c) decide how to implement the best option, (d) quantify or rank the alternatives.   4. _____

5. The final step in the problem-solving model is to (a) take action, (b) evaluate alternatives and select the best option, (c) evaluate the action, (d) identify various solutions.   5. _____

6. Good communication is important in the problem-solving process because when trying to resolve problems and make decisions, you will likely need to (a) interact with others, (b) request information and express your ideas, (c) listen to suggestions from others, (d) all of these.   6. _____

7. Brainstorming (a) involves discussing a large number of ideas, (b) is used to analyze practical ideas, (c) is a creative problem-solving technique, (d) none of these.   7. _____

8. In a brainstorming session, you should (a) write down only solutions that seem practical, (b) come up with as many ideas as possible, (c) evaluate each idea as soon as it is proposed, (d) always work with at least two other trusted colleagues.   8. _____

9. From an entrepreneur's perspective, mistakes (a) have no place in the problem-solving process, (b) will never be made if the problem-solving process is correctly followed, (c) should be viewed as a learning experience, (d) are always a negative.   9. _____

Problem Solving

Directions   Answer the following questions in the space provided.

1. List three places where you can find relevant information in the second step of the problem-solving model.

   _____

   _____

   _____

   _____

   _____

2. Select one of your answers to Question 1 and describe a situation in which the information obtained would be relevant.

   _____

   _____

   _____

   _____

   _____

3. The last step in the problem-solving model is evaluating the action. Explain what an entrepreneur could do if this evaluation showed that the action did not solve the problem.

   _____

   _____

   _____

   _____

   _____

4. Explain why good communication is important in the problem-solving process.

   _____

   _____

   _____

   _____

   _____

5. Describe how brainstorming could be used in the problem-solving model.

   _____

   _____

   _____

   _____

   _____

Entrepreneurship: Ideas in Action, 6e, Student Edition

Chapter 1 Assessment
Should You Become an Entrepreneur?

Vocabulary Review

Directions   In the Answers column, write the letter that represents the word, or group of words, that correctly completes the statements.

Answers

1. People who own, operate, and take the risk of a business venture

2. The process of running a business of one's own

3. People hired to work for someone else

4. An evaluation of your strengths and weaknesses

5. The ability to learn a particular kind of job

6. Special meetings where companies of the same industry or related industries display their products

7. A creative problem-solving technique that involves generating a large number of fresh ideas

8. Possibilities that arise from existing conditions

9. Thoughts or concepts that come from creative thinking

a. aptitude
b. brainstorming
c. employees
d. entrepreneurs
e. entrepreneurship
f. ideas
g. opportunities
h. self-assessment
i. trade shows

1. _____
2. _____
3. _____
4. _____
5. _____
6. _____
7. _____
8. _____
9. _____

Fill-in-the-Blank

Directions   For each item below, determine the word(s) that best complete the sentence. Write the word(s) in the Answers column.

Answers

1. Entrepreneurs try to identify unmet _____ of the marketplace.

2. _____ businesses sell products directly to the people who use or consume them.

3. If it is not possible to quantify the alternatives in the fourth step of the problem-solving model, the decision maker may _____ each alternative.

4. Successful entrepreneurs are _____-oriented.

5. To assess your suitability for entrepreneurship, you should consider your strengths, weaknesses, _____, interests, past experiences, and aptitude.

6. An advantage of entrepreneurship is that entrepreneurs are their own _____.

7. Goals should be _____, or represent things to which you are willing to commit.

8. In comparing different business opportunities, you should look at the particular _____ associated with the business.

9. How much money you want to earn is a(n) _____ goal.

10. The first step in the problem-solving model is to _____ the problem.

11. When operating with _____, entrepreneurs behave consistently in actions, values, methods, measures, principles, expectations, and outcomes.

12. Attending conferences, seminars, and workshops enable entrepreneurs to _____.

13. Many entrepreneurs make decisions casually or base them on _____.

1. _____
2. _____
3. _____
4. _____
5. _____
6. _____
7. _____
8. _____
9. _____
10. _____
11. _____
12. _____
13. _____

Problem Solving

Directions   Answer the following questions in the spaces provided.

1. For everything you do in life, you set goals. Goals help you stay on track and follow through with your plans. The best goals are SMART. SMART goals provide more direction for you.

   In the table below, define each component of a SMART goal. Then write a personal goal you have for yourself. Finally, rewrite your goal as a SMART goal.

SMART Goals	
SMART Goal Components	**Definition**
Specific	
Measurable	
Attainable	
Realistic	
Timely	
Goal:	
SMART Goal:	

2. For the SMART goal you have identified above, list five specific tasks that will help you achieve these goals and assign a deadline to each.

Task	Completion Date

2.1 Entrepreneurs Satisfy Needs and Wants

True or False

Directions Place a *T* for True or an *F* for False in the Answers column to show whether each of the following statements is true or false.

Answers

1. Needs are things that you must have in order to survive. 1._____

2. The role of businesses is to produce and distribute goods and services that people need and want. 2._____

3. The most basic of needs is security. 3._____

4. Both types of wants—economic and noneconomic—form the basis of an economy. 4._____

5. Needs and wants are unlimited. 5._____

6. Economic resources are not factors of production. 6._____

7. Services must be provided to you at the time you need them—they cannot be stored. 7._____

8. Capital resources include buildings and equipment. 8._____

9. All economic resources have a limited supply. 9._____

10. All businesses that exist in the United States today began as an entrepreneurial idea. 10._____

Multiple Choice

Directions In the Answers column, write the letter that represents the word, or group of words, that correctly completes the statement.

Answers

1. Needs include all of the following *except* (a) food, (b) smartphones, (c) basic clothing, (d) a place to live. 1._____

2. Things that you think you must have in order to be satisfied are called (a) needs, (b) preferences, (c) goals, (d) wants. 2._____

3. The psychologist who developed a theory on the hierarchy of needs was (a) Abraham Maslow, (b) Sigmund Freud, (c) Karl Jung, (d) Terrence McKenna. 3._____

4. According to the theory of hierarchy of needs, (a) everyone's needs will eventually be satisfied, (b) people must satisfy lower-level needs before they can focus on higher-level needs, (c) everyone has the same needs, (d) needs and wants are usually the same. 4._____

5. Earning a college degree is an example of satisfying which of the following areas of needs? (a) Esteem, (b) Social, (c) Self-actualization, (d) Security. 5._____

6. Products you can see and touch are called (a) services, (b) goods, (c) intangibles, (d) all of these. 6._____

7. The three types of economic resources that an entrepreneur may use to create useful goods and services are called (a) factors of production (b) economies of scale, (c) factors of consumption, (d) production hierarchies. 7._____

8. Raw materials supplied by nature are (a) human resources, (b) capital resources, (c) natural resources, (d) monetary resources. 8._____

9. Which of the following would *not* be considered a capital resource? (a) Buildings, (b) Equipment, (c) The money needed to pay employees, (d) Employees. 9._____

10. In the U.S. economy, entrepreneurs (a) fulfill consumers' wants and needs, (b) provide employment, (c) help change the way people live and conduct business, (d) all of these. 10._____

Problem Solving

Directions   Answer the following questions in the space provided.

1. In the following hierarchy of needs, correctly list each need and provide an example of each.

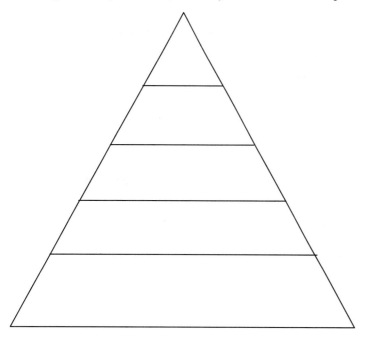

2. In the table below, list at least three needs in your own life. Then indicate where each ranks on the hierarchy of needs.

Need	Rank on Hierarchy

Name _____ Class _____ Date _____

2.2 How Economic Decisions Are Made

True or False

Directions Place a *T* for True or an *F* for False in the Answers column to show whether each of the following statements is true or false.

Answers

1. Entrepreneurship thrives in a market economy.   1._____

2. The traditional economy is used in developed countries.   2._____

3. A mixed economy often results when a country shifts away from a command economy toward a market economy.   3._____

4. The U.S. economic system is best described as a traditional economy.   4._____

5. The rivalry among businesses to sell their goods and services is called competition.   5._____

6. Two factors that commonly enter into economic decision making are scarcity and opportunity cost.   6._____

7. The value of the next-best economic alternative is the trade-off cost.   7._____

8. The functions of business operate independently of each other.   8._____

9. The primary reason a business exists in a market economy is to earn a profit.   9._____

Multiple Choice

Directions   In the Answers column, write the letter that represents the word, or group of words, that correctly completes the statement.

Answers

1. Which of the following is *not* one of the three basic questions that all economies must answer? (a) What goods and services will be produced? (b) How will the goods and services be produced? (c) When will the goods and services be produced? (d) For whom will the goods and services be produced?   1._____

2. In a command economy, (a) there is very little choice for consumers in what is available, (b) individuals may not always be able to obtain exactly what they want, (c) the government determines what, how, and for whom goods are produced, (d) all of these.   2._____

3. In a market economy, individual choice (a) does not influence how items are produced, (b) creates the market for a good or service, (c) has no effect on production, (d) creates scarcity.   3._____

4. Today, China operates under a (a) mixed economy, (b) traditional economy, (c) market economy, (d) command economy.   4._____

5. The U.S. economic system is based on all of the following principles *except* (a) private property, (b) freedom of choice, (c) government control, (d) competition.   5._____

6. In the U.S. economy, competition forces a business to (a) improve products, (b) keep costs low, (c) provide good customer service, (d) all of these.   6._____

7. Scarcity exists because (a) there are different types of economies, (b) there are too many people in the world, (c) resources are limited, (d) some products are expensive to produce.   7._____

8. All of the following are a function of business *except* (a) production, (b) management, (c) opportunity cost, (d) finance.   8._____

9. All of the following are components of the marketing mix *except* (a) product, (b) distribution, (c) competition, (d) price.   9._____

Problem Solving

Directions   Answer the following questions in the space provided.

1. Explain the difference between a command economy and a market economy.

_____

_____

_____

_____

_____

_____

_____

_____

_____

2. Explain the four basic principles upon which the U.S. economy is based. Which of these principles do you think is the most distinctly "American"? Explain your answer.

_____

_____

_____

_____

_____

_____

_____

_____

3. Identify at least three businesses in your community that are competitors. Which of these businesses do you prefer? Why?

_____

_____

_____

_____

_____

_____

_____

_____

_____

Entrepreneurship: Ideas in Action, 6e, Student Edition

2.3 What Affects Price?

True or False

Directions Place a *T* for True or an *F* for False in the Answers column to show whether
each of the following statements is true or false.

Answers

1. The supply curve for a market economy shows that as the price of a product or service
    rises, suppliers are willing to produce more of the good or service.

    1._____

2. The demand curve for a market economy shows that as the price of a product or service
    rises, individuals are willing to consume more of the good or service.

    2._____

3. Demand elasticity occurs when demand for a product is affected by its price.

    3._____

4. Inelastic demand occurs when a change in price creates more demand.

    4._____

5. Fixed costs must be paid even if a company has no sales.

    5._____

6. When the quantity of a good or service produced increases, variable costs remain the
    same.

    6._____

7. Marginal benefit measures the advantages of producing one additional unit of a good or
    service.

    7._____

8. In a market with perfect competition, a small number of businesses gain the majority of
    total sales revenue.

    8._____

9. It is difficult for new businesses to enter a market with an oligopoly market structure.

    9._____

Multiple Choice

Directions In the Answers column, write the letter that represents the word, or group of
words, that correctly completes the statement.

Answers

1. A supply curve shows that the quantity produced (a) increases as price decreases,
    (b) increases as price increases, (c) decreases as price increases, (d) is not affected by
    price.

    1._____

2. A demand curve shows that the quantity consumed (a) increases as price decreases,
    (b) increases as price increases, (c) decreases as price decreases, (d) is not affected by
    price.

    2._____

3. The fixed costs of a business (a) include monthly rent, (b) are based on the price of
    supplies, (c) do not include the cost of insurance, (d) include advertising costs.

    3._____

4. If an entrepreneur's variable cost for each unit produced is $1.35, how much would the
    fixed costs increase if 30 additional units were demanded each day? (a) $40.50 per day,
    (b) $40.50 per week, (c) $202.50 per week, (d) none of these.

    4._____

5. When a business owner decides to grow the business he or she needs to consider the
    (a) equilibrium quantity, (b) variable costs, (c) marginal cost, (d) economies of scale.

    5._____

6. Market structures are distinguished by all of the following *except* (a) the types of goods
    and services being traded, (b) the amount of profit that can be earned by sellers, (c) the
    barriers to entry into the market for sellers, (d) the number and size of sellers and
    buyers in the market.

    6._____

7. Which of the following is *not* one of the four major market structures? (a) Perfect
    competition, (b) Monopoly, (c) Oligopoly, (d) Pure competition.

    7._____

8. Which of the following market structures are retail stores and restaurants found in?
    (a) Oligopoly, (b) Perfect competition, (c) Monopolistic competition, (d) None of these.

    8._____

Problem Solving

Directions   Answer the following questions in the spaces provided.

1. Describe what a supply curve looks like.

    _____

    _____

    _____

    _____

    _____

2. Explain why a supply curve looks the way it does.

    _____

    _____

    _____

    _____

    _____

3. Describe what a demand curve looks like.

    _____

    _____

    _____

    _____

    _____

4. Explain why a demand curve looks the way it does.

    _____

    _____

    _____

    _____

    _____

5. What is the significance of the intersection point of the supply and demand curves for a product or service?

    _____

    _____

    _____

    _____

    _____

Chapter 2 Assessment
Entrepreneurs in a Market Economy

Vocabulary Review

Directions   In the space provided, write a sentence that correctly uses each of the following terms. Your sentence should *not* be a definition of the term.

1. equilibrium price

2. monopoly

3. variable costs

4. natural resources

Fill-in-the-Blank

Directions   For each item below, determine the word(s) that best complete the sentence. Write the word(s) in the Answers column.

Answers

1. Communism is an example of a(n) _____ economy.

   1._____

2. The _____ function of business creates or obtains products or services for sale.

   2._____

3. _____ measures the advantages of producing one additional unit of a good or service.

   3._____

4. _____ is another name for the economic system in the United States.

   4._____

5. An entrepreneur who chooses one alternative over another is using the concept of _____ cost.

   5._____

6. When a market is dominated by a small number of businesses that gain the majority of total sales revenue, it is called a(n) _____.

   6._____

7. _____ are activities that are consumed as they are produced.

   7._____

8. The people who create goods and services are called _____ resources.

   8._____

9. A market with _____ competition consists of a very large number of businesses producing nearly identical products and has many buyers.

   9._____

10. _____ occurs when individual workers focus on single tasks, enabling each worker to become more efficient and productive.

    10._____

Problem Solving

Directions   Answer the following questions. Show your work and write your answers in the spaces provided.

1. At a price of $7.95 each, a nursery sells 60 one-gallon plants a day. The owner hopes to increase total revenue by changing the price of these plants. Find the total revenue for each price shown in the following table.

Price	Number Sold per Day	Total Revenue per Day
$6.95	70	
$7.49	65	
$7.95	60	
$8.49	55	

Should the nursery owner change the price of the plants? Explain your answer.

_____

_____

_____

_____

_____

2. The owner of a specialty delicatessen buys baskets, decorates and fills them with food items, and sells them as one of the products in the shop. The entrepreneur sells an average of 130 baskets a month. The basket supplier charges $0.50 per basket. The entrepreneur would like to reduce his variable costs and has found a basket supplier who will charge only $0.40 per basket. How much will the delicatessen owner save in a year by changing suppliers?

_____

_____

_____

_____

3. An entrepreneur makes a part used in the auto industry that he sells for $2.65 each. Yearly sales of this part have been 20,400 a year for the last three years. The customer has cut production and has reduced its purchase of these parts by 35 percent. How much yearly revenue will the entrepreneur lose as a result?

_____

_____

_____

_____

_____

3.1 Why a Business Plan Is Important

True or False

Directions Place a *T* for True or an *F* for False in the Answers column to show whether each of the following statements is true or false.

Answers

1. A business plan provides detailed financial information that shows how your business will succeed in earning a profit.

1._____

2. Writing a business plan is one of the easiest things you will do as an entrepreneur.

2._____

3. To convince investors that the idea is solid, you will need a completely new product or service or one that is less expensive than products or services that already exist.

3._____

4. A good business plan should describe what products or services will be introduced over the next five years.

4._____

5. The backgrounds and experience of the leadership team of your company help lenders make financing decisions.

5._____

6. Not all new businesses need a business plan.

6._____

7. Lenders require a business plan before they will consider financing a business.

7._____

8. Once your business is up and running, you will rarely use your business plan.

8._____

Multiple Choice

Directions In the Answers column, write the letter that represents the word, or group of words, that correctly completes the statement.

Answers

1. A business plan should (a) explain who will supply your business with goods, (b) show how your business will win over customers from competitors, (c) explain who will run your business, (d) all of these.

1._____

2. A business plan explains how your product or service (a) will be produced, (b) will be sold, (c) is either new or better than existing products or services, (d) all of these.

2._____

3. Long-term sales projections are (a) for two to four years after startup, (b) for five years in the future, (c) for ten years in the future, (d) not included in a business plan.

3._____

4. Before lenders will loan money to a new business, (a) they will want to interview all potential employees, (b) the new business must have at least two years' worth of work already lined up, (c) they need to be convinced that the leadership team of the business have the skills and characteristics necessary to succeed, (d) all of these.

4._____

5. Which of the following is *not* a purpose of a business plan? (a) To describe the backgrounds and experience of your suppliers, (b) To explain the idea behind your business, (c) To explain how you expect to achieve specific objectives, (d) To describe the backgrounds and experience of the leadership team of the business.

5._____

6. Before they will consider financing a business, lenders require (a) an organizational chart that lists all of your employees, (b) a business plan, (c) the history and background of your product, (d) all of these.

6._____

7. Working on a business plan helps you (a) think through business strategies, (b) identify problems that you may encounter, (c) recognize limits, (d) all of these.

7._____

8. A business plan is important for all of the following reasons *except* (a) it helps you communicate your ideas to others, (b) it helps you decide what to sell, (c) it can help you secure financing for your business, (d) it makes you think about all aspects of your business.

8._____

Problem Solving

Directions   Answer the following questions in the space provided.

1. Explain how the three purposes of a business plan apply to obtaining financing for a new business.

_____

_____

_____

_____

_____

_____

_____

_____

2. Explain how the three purposes of a business plan apply to starting a new business if the entrepreneur does not need financing.

_____

_____

_____

_____

_____

_____

_____

_____

3. Explain why a business plan is important for every new business.

_____

_____

_____

_____

_____

_____

_____

_____

3.2 What Goes Into a Business Plan?

True or False

Directions Place a *T* for True or an *F* for False in the Answers column to show whether each of the following statements is true or false.

Answers

1. Regardless of the business, all business plans serve the same basic purposes. 1._____

2. Only corporations need to include a section detailing the form of ownership in a business plan. 2._____

3. The marketing section of your business plan should describe the location of your business. 3._____

4. A financial statement based on projected revenues and expenses is called an informal financial statement. 4._____

5. The financial management section of your business plan should state how much money you need to borrow and how you plan to use the money. 5._____

6. A brief explanation of why you are asking for a loan and what you plan to do with the money is called an executive summary. 6._____

7. The executive summary appears after the body of the business plan. 7._____

8. A handwritten business plan is acceptable if it is neat, well organized, and inviting to read. 8._____

Multiple Choice

Directions In the Answers column, write the letter that represents the word, or group of words, that correctly completes the statement.

Answers

1. The introduction section of a business plan contains all of the following *except* (a) a description of the nature of the business, (b) the legal structure of the business, (c) an identification of risks, (d) the advantages your business has over your competitors. 1._____

2. The marketing section of your plan explains (a) how you plan to enter the market, (b) who your prospective customers are, (c) how you plan to deal with competition, (d) all of these. 2._____

3. Which of the following is *not* an element of the financial management section of your plan? (a) Identification of risks, (b) Distribution of profits and losses, (c) Financial statements, (d) Funding request and return on investment. 3._____

4. In the financial management section of its business plan, a new business must include (a) projected financial statements, (b) copies of all rental agreements, (c) current financial statements, (d) all of these. 4._____

5. Information about necessary equipment for your business is included in a business plan's (a) financial management section, (b) concluding statement, (c) marketing section, (d) operations section. 5._____

6. A business plan's title page includes all of the following *except* (a) a brief description of the business, (b) the name of the company, (c) the date, (d) the owner's name. 6._____

7. An executive summary (a) should be written before the business plan is completed, (b) includes supporting documents that back up statements made in the body of the report, (c) states how much you want to borrow, (d) should be no longer than one or two paragraphs. 7._____

8. The appendix of a business plan might include (a) tax returns of the business owner, (b) letters of recommendation, (c) a copy of required licenses, (d) all of these. 8._____

Problem Solving

Directions   Answer the following questions in the space provided.

1. In the marketing section of your business plan, you need to provide information in four areas.

    a. What information should be included about your products or services?

    _____

    _____

    _____

    b. What information should be included about your market?

    _____

    _____

    _____

    _____

    c. What information should be included about the industry you will operate in?

    _____

    _____

    _____

    d. How might the location of your business affect its success?

    _____

    _____

    _____

2. The financial management section of your business plan consists of three elements. List these elements, describe what is included in each, and explain why the information is necessary.

    _____

    _____

    _____

    _____

    _____

    _____

    _____

    _____

    _____

    _____

    _____

    _____

3.3 How to Create an Effective Business Plan

True or False

Directions Place a *T* for True or an *F* for False in the Answers column to show whether each of the following statements is true or false.

Answers

1. To convince readers that you have come up with a practical business idea, you must include information and data from objective sources.

    1._____

2. The Small Business Administration (SBA) has at least one office in every U.S. state.

    2._____

3. SCORE is cosponsored by the SBA.

    3._____

4. Entrepreneurs can hire experts from trade associations to help them prepare business plans.

    4._____

5. A local chamber of commerce can provide information on trends affecting local businesses, local resources, and zoning and licensing information.

    5._____

6. The Internet is not a trusted source of information on how to develop a business plan.

    6._____

7. An undefined target market can ruin a business plan.

    7._____

8. Never reveal your competitors' strengths in your business plan—focus only on what they have done wrong.

    8._____

9. The only person who should read a business plan is the owner and potential investors.

    9._____

Multiple Choice

Directions In the Answers column, write the letter that represents the word, or group of words, that correctly completes the statement.

Answers

1. The SBA (a) is an independent agency of the federal government, (b) provides loans and loan guarantees to entrepreneurs and small businesses, (c) has at least one office in every U.S. state, (d) all of these.

    1._____

2. Small Business Development Centers (SBDCs) (a) are often located at community and state colleges, (b) are made up of working and retired business professionals, (c) provide real-world advice and know-how for a small fee, (d) all of these.

    2._____

3. SCORE is (a) cosponsored by the federal government, (b) a for-profit association, (c) an independent agency of the federal government, (d) made up of working and retired business professionals.

    3._____

4. Trade associations provide all of the following to entrepreneurs *except* (a) valuable information, (b) education, (c) networking opportunities, (d) small loans.

    4._____

5. Which of the following is *least* likely to be a helpful resource for your business plan? (a) *National Geographic*, (b) books on entrepreneurship, (c) SBA publications, (d) *Entrepreneur* magazine.

    5._____

6. Online business resources (a) should not be used in a business plan, (b) are not as reliable as print resources, (c) can be found via search engines, (d) are not available from the SBA.

    6._____

7. Financial projections in a business plan should (a) not be included if you could not locate reliable financial information, (b) be based on solid evidence, (c) be very optimistic so that investors will be impressed, (d) based on your best guess.

    7._____

8. Your business plan must (a) clearly define your market, (b) never overlook the competition, (c) be consistent, (d) all of these.

    8._____

Problem Solving

Directions   Answer the following questions in the space provided.

1. List five organizations that can be used as resources to obtain information or assistance for preparing a business plan.

   _____

   _____

   _____

   _____

   _____

2. Describe the types of print resources that are available to help you research a business plan and where you can obtain them.

   _____

   _____

   _____

   _____

   _____

3. Describe the types of online resources that are available to help you research a business plan.

   _____

   _____

   _____

   _____

   _____

4. List five common mistakes that are often made when creating a business plan, and state how these mistakes can be avoided.

   _____

   _____

   _____

   _____

   _____

   _____

   _____

   _____

   _____

   _____

Chapter 3 Assessment
Develop a Business Plan

Vocabulary Review

Directions   In each of the following sentences, the underlined term is not used correctly, In the space provided, rewrite the sentence so the term is used correctly.

1. A <u>business plan</u> is a handwritten document that lists all the steps necessary in operating a business.

2. In the history and background section of a business plan, an entrepreneur should include <u>pro forma financial statements</u>, which are statements of the funding request and return on investment.

3. <u>Trade associations</u> are organizations that exist to provide loans, loan guarantees, contracts, counseling sessions, and other forms of assistance to entrepreneurs and small businesses.

Fill-in-the-Blank

Directions   For each item below, determine the word(s) that best complete the sentence. Write the word(s) in the Answers column.

Answers

1. Medium-term sales projections cover a period of about _____ years.

    1. _____

2. A business plan may help you secure _____ for your business.

    2. _____

3. A description of the industry in which you will operate your business is found in the _____ section of a business plan.

    3. _____

4. The _____ section of a business plan discusses hiring and personnel procedures.

    4. _____

5. A common mistake made by many entrepreneurs is to provide _____ financial projections in their business plans.

    5. _____

6. _____ is a nonprofit association made up of working and retired business professionals who volunteer their time to provide small businesses and entrepreneurs with free real-world advice and know-how.

    6. _____

7. The _____ for your business plan should briefly describe your business, its potential for success, and the amount of capital you need.

    7. _____

8. A business plan must provide detailed financial information that shows how your business will succeed in earning a(n) _____.

    8. _____

9. In the concluding statement of a business plan, you should emphasize your commitment to the _____ of the business.

    9. _____

10. A(n) _____ is the way an entrepreneur intends to extract his or her money from a business after it is operating successfully.

    10. _____

Problem Solving

Directions Answer the following questions. Write your answers in the spaces provided.

1. In the first column of the following table, list the introductory elements of a business plan in the order in which they should appear. In the second column, describe the physical characteristics of each element, such as length, format, and so on. In the third column, describe what the element should include. The first element is listed as an example.

Introductory Element	Physical Characteristics	Contents
Cover letter	*One-page letter on letterhead, word processed on standard-size paper*	*Name, address, phone number, and email address of the owner; name of the business; brief description of the business and its potential for success; amount of capital needed*

2. Describe what should be included in the appendix of a business plan.

_____

_____

_____

_____

_____

_____

_____

_____

4.1   Identify Your Market

True or False

Directions   Place a *T* for True or an *F* for False in the Answers column to show whether each of the following statements is true or false.

Answers

1. To guarantee success for your business, you must come up with a good business idea.   1. _____

2. Entrepreneurs estimate demand for their products or services by identifying their target market.   2. _____

3. Marital status, income, and age are useful data for identifying your target market.   3. _____

4. A market segment is made up of people who share common characteristics.   4. _____

5. Segmenting your target market is usually not necessary because most markets are small.   5. _____

6. Data that helps you determine how often potential customers use a particular service is called a customer profile.   6. _____

7. A customer profile should include demographic data but not psychographic data.   7. _____

8. A marketing strategy identifies customers that you can serve more effectively than your competitors can, but it cannot help you determine the size of your market.   8. _____

9. Demographics describe a group of people in terms of their tastes, opinions, personality traits, and lifestyle habits.   9. _____

Multiple Choice

Directions   In the Answers column, write the letter that represents the word, or group of words, that correctly completes the statement.

Answers

1. The customers you would most like to attract are referred to as your (a) competition, (b) market segments, (c) target market, (d) demographics.   1. _____

2. Which of the following would *most* likely be the target market for a car dealer selling moderately priced minivans? (a) Single people with higher incomes, (b) Middle-class families with children, (c) People who are retired, (d) None of these.   2. _____

3. By continually evaluating your market, you can be ready to respond to changes in all of the following *except* (a) government, (b) communities, (c) consumer tastes, (d) competitors' offerings.   3. _____

4. Most products and services appeal to (a) a large portion of the population, (b) the demographic market, (c) a market segment, (d) none of these.   4. _____

5. A description of the characteristics of the person or company that is likely to purchase a product or service is a (a) target market, (b) customer profile, (c) psychographic profile, (d) demographic summary.   5. _____

6. Demographics are data that describe a group of people in terms of their (a) income, (b) tastes, (c) opinions, (d) needs.   6. _____

7. Psychographics are data that describe a group of people in terms of their (a) lifestyle habits, (b) personality traits, (c) opinions, (d) all of these.   7. _____

8. Data that help you determine how often potential customers use a particular service are called (a) geographic data, (b) demographics, (c) psychographics, (d) use-based data.   8. _____

9. Data that help you determine where your potential customers live and how far they will travel to do business with you are called (a) use-based data, (b) geographic data, (c) census data, (d) secondary data.   9. _____

Problem Solving

Directions Answer the following questions in the space provided.

1. Describe the difference between demographics and psychographics.

   _____

   _____

   _____

   _____

   _____

   _____

2. How do demographics and psychographics relate to identifying your target market?

   _____

   _____

   _____

   _____

   _____

   _____

3. An entrepreneur developed the following customer profile for her pet store. Which of the information in the profile is demographic data? Psychographic data? Geographic data?

   _____

   _____

   _____

   _____

CUSTOMER PROFILE FOR A PET STORE
• Individual or couple 25 to 55 years of age
• Own one or more pets
• One or both members of household work full-time in professional field
• Want high-quality pet foods and accessories
• Willing to pay high prices for high quality
• Live in exclusive city residential area
• Average household income: $135,000 per year

   _____

   _____

   _____

4. List ten market segments for the retail clothing market.

   _____

   _____

   _____

   _____

   _____

Entrepreneurship: Ideas in Action, 6e, Student Edition

4.2   Research the Market

True or False

Directions   Place a *T* for True or an *F* for False in the Answers column to show whether
each of the following statements is true or false.

Answers

1. Information collected for the very first time to fit a specific purpose is primary data.

    1. _____

2. Surveys should be kept to a page in length when read over the phone or mailed to respondents.

    2. _____

3. Focus groups are quick interviews with target customers.

    3. _____

4. Collecting primary data can be expensive and time-consuming.

    4. _____

5. The first step in conducting primary market research is to select a research method.

    5. _____

6. Observation is the best research method if you want to find out people's opinions.

    6. _____

7. Economic trends and industry forecasts help determine the kind of primary data research to perform.

    7. _____

8. The movement of data between locations in a structured, computer-retrievable format is known as electronic data mining.

    8. _____

9. The goal of social media marketing is to product content that users will share with their social network to help a company reach more customers.

    9. _____

Multiple Choice

Directions   In the Answers column, write the letter that represents the word, or group of
words, that correctly completes the statement.

Answers

1. Which of the following is *not* a way to collect primary data? (a) Focus groups, (b) Consumer opinion blogs, (c) Surveys, (d) Observation.

    1. _____

2. A good survey should (a) have easy-to-answer questions, (b) be at least two pages long, (c) explain in detail why you are conducting the survey, (d) all of these.

    2. _____

3. Secondary data are found (a) in government publications, (b) on the Internet, (c) in newspapers, (d) all of these.

    3. _____

4. In the first step in the market research process, you need to (a) determine what data you need to collect, (b) define the market research question, (c) decide how you will gather data, (d) determine how much data you will need to collect.

    4. _____

5. In designing a survey, you should consider all of the following *except* (a) length of the survey, (b) how you plan to administer it, (c) when you can get the best information, (d) the purpose of each question.

    5. _____

6. Customer relationship management focuses on (a) understanding customers as individuals (b) understanding customers as part of a group, (c) identifying a target market, (d) none of these.

    6. _____

7. Which of the following is *not* an example of a touch point? (a) a product registration form, (b) the return of a completed warranty card, (c) a request for product information, (d) an order of goods from a supplier.

    7. _____

8. Finding hidden patterns and relationships in customer data is called data (a) mining, (b) warehousing, (c) collection, (d) evaluation.

    8. _____

9. Social media marketing (a) helps a company get indirect feedback from customers, (b) is a useful but expensive way to promote a product, (c) is a good way for companies to increase exposure, (d) has failed to catch on because not everyone uses social media.

    9. _____

Problem Solving

Directions   The three primary data research methods are listed below. For each, give a brief description of the method, explain the situation in which it would be used, and list some advantages and disadvantages of the method. Write your answers in the space provided.

1. Survey

_____

_____

_____

_____

_____

_____

_____

_____

2. Observation

_____

_____

_____

_____

_____

_____

_____

_____

_____

3. Focus group

_____

_____

_____

_____

_____

_____

_____

_____

_____

4.3 Know Your Competition

True or False

Directions   Place a *T* for True or an *F* for False in the Answers column to show whether each of the following statements is true or false.

Answers

1. Businesses typically enter into areas where there is competition.   1._____

2. Secondary data resources and observation methods can help you learn about your direct competition.   2._____

3. Your indirect competition are those businesses that make most of their money selling products or services that are the same as or similar to yours.   3._____

4. One reason why small entrepreneurs can compete successfully with large retailers is because large retail chains carry more than one product line.   4._____

5. Your analysis of competitors should include their prices, locations, and facilities.   5._____

6. A competitor's strengths should be viewed as threats to your business.   6._____

7. To retain customers, you will need to occasionally ask them for their opinions about your business and respond to their feedback.   7._____

8. Superior service and frequent-buyer programs are strategies you can use to maintain customer loyalty.   8._____

Multiple Choice

Directions   In the Answers column, write the letter that represents the word, or group of words, that correctly completes the statement.

Answers

1. All of the following can provide information about direct competition *except* (a) the U.S. Postal Service, (b) the Internet, (c) your local chamber of commerce, (d) observation methods.   1._____

2. Which of the following would be considered an indirect competitor of McDonald's? (a) Kentucky Fried Chicken, (b) Pizza Hut, (c) Subway, (d) all of these.   2._____

3. As an entrepreneur, you may find that indirect competitors (a) are more difficult to locate than direct competitors, (b) are usually located in malls or shopping centers, (c) make most of their money selling the same or similar products or services that you sell, (d) none of these.   3._____

4. Small businesses may have difficulty competing with large retailers because large retailers (a) develop more complete customer profiles, (b) are able to keep larger quantities of products in stock, (c) have a larger target market, (d) offer superior service.   4._____

5. A competitive analysis does all of the following *except* (a) identify competitors, (b) summarize the products and prices offered by competitors, (c) identify threats from a competitor, (d) research a competitor's business plan.   5._____

6. Competitors should be analyzed concerning their (a) prices, (b) locations, (c) strengths and weaknesses, (d) all of these.   6._____

7. The main purpose of customer loyalty strategies is to (a) obtain new customers, (b) keep customers happy so that they return to the business, (c) save money, (d) none of these.   7._____

8. All of the following are strategies designed to maintain customer loyalty *except* (a) providing store-specific credit cards, (b) locating in a city center, (c) having easy return policies, (d) having more convenient hours than other businesses.   8._____

Problem Solving

Directions   Answer the following questions in the space provided.

1. How might the competition in a rural area or small town be different than the competition in a large metropolitan area?

_____

_____

_____

_____

_____

2. How does analyzing the strengths and weaknesses of specific competitors help an entrepreneur?

_____

_____

_____

_____

_____

3. What might an entrepreneur do to compete with mail-order businesses that sell the same product?

_____

_____

_____

_____

_____

4. What strategies can owners of small businesses use to compete with large retailers?

_____

_____

_____

_____

_____

5. What is the most important way to maintain customer loyalty?

_____

_____

_____

_____

_____

Entrepreneurship: Ideas in Action, 6e, Student Edition

Chapter 4 Assessment
Identify and Meet a Market Need

Vocabulary Review

Directions In the space provided, write a sentence that correctly uses each of the following terms. Your sentence should *not* be a definition of the term.

1. demographics

2. secondary data

3. focus group

4. direct competition

Fill-in-the-Blank

Directions For each item below, determine the word(s) that best complete the sentence. Write the word(s) in the Answers column.

Answers

1. Identifying your _____ market helps you reach the people who desire your products and services.

   1. _____

2. _____ are the people or organizations who buy the products and services that businesses offer.

   2. _____

3. _____ is a system for collecting, recording, and analyzing information about customers, competitors, products, and services.

   3. _____

4. A description of the characteristics of the person or company that is likely to purchase a product or service is a(n) _____.

   4. _____

5. Market _____ are groups of customers within a large market who share common characteristics.

   5. _____

6. An opportunity exists for an entrepreneur when a customer need is going unmet by a(n) _____.

   6. _____

7. Information collected for the first time by observation or surveys is _____ data.

   7. _____

8. A(n) _____ can be read over the phone or mailed to respondents.

   8. _____

9. _____ is the last step in the market research process.

   9. _____

10. Competition by a business that makes only a small amount of money selling the same or similar products or services as another business is _____ competition.

    10. _____

Problem Solving

Directions Answer the following questions in the space provided.

1. List at least six questions an entrepreneur needs to answer in order to identify the target market for his or her product or service.

_____

_____

_____

_____

_____

_____

_____

_____

_____

_____

_____

_____

2. Describe the types of demographic and psychographic data that are available in secondary data resources and that can be useful in market research.

_____

_____

_____

_____

_____

_____

3. In the table below, identify a business you patronize frequently. Then list all of the direct competitors of this business you can think of—local, national, or online.

Business You Patronize	Direct Competitors

Entrepreneurship: Ideas in Action, 6e, Student Edition

5.1   Develop the Marketing Plan

True or False

Directions   Place a *T* for True or an *F* for False in the Answers column to show whether each of the following statements is true or false.

Answers

1. The marketing concept for a business is developed by using the primary and secondary data that is gathered through market research.

    1._____

2. The marketing concept uses the needs of the business as the primary focus during the planning, production, distribution, and promotion of a product or service.

    2._____

3. Establishing short-, medium-, and long-term marketing goals ensures that the marketing you do today fits the vision you have for your business tomorrow.

    3._____

4. Short-term goals should not be listed in terms of product, price, distribution, and promotion.

    4._____

5. Long-term goals describe what you want your business to achieve in the next two or three years.

    5._____

6. Long-term goals show where you would like your business to be five or ten years from now but do not help you think about how to market your business today.

    6._____

7. You should develop a marketing plan before setting short-, medium-, and long-term goals for your business.

    7._____

8. The marketing plan should be separate from your business plan.

    8._____

Multiple Choice

Directions   In the Answers column, write the letter that represents the word, or group of words, that correctly completes the statement.

Answers

1. Marketing consists of all of the following processes *except* (a) pricing, (b) operating, (c) selling, (d) promoting.

    1._____

2. To use the marketing concept, businesses must do all of the following *except* (a) identify what will satisfy customers' needs and wants, (b) operate profitably, (c) devote half of its profits toward marketing, (d) develop and market products that customers consider better than other choices.

    2._____

3. Your marketing strategy should address (a) product introduction or innovation, (b) pricing, (c) market share, (d) all of these.

    3._____

4. Marketing goals (a) need to be established only for the long-term, (b) should never change, (c) can be used to determine your product mix, (d) none of these.

    4._____

5. Short-term goals can be stated in terms of (a) number of customers, (b) level of profits, (c) level of sales, (d) all of these.

    5._____

6. Medium-term goals describe what you want your business to achieve (a) in the next ten years, (b) in terms of market share, (c) in the next two to five years, (d) by using various promotion methods.

    6._____

7. A long-term goal might be to (a) expand by adding a second location, (b) increase market share to 50 percent, (c) establish a customer base, (d) network with other business owners.

    7._____

8. A marketing plan should do all of the following *except* (a) identify your competitors, (b) outline a strategy for keeping customers, (c) identify the owner's net worth, (d) recognize and anticipate change.

    8._____

Problem Solving

Directions Answer the following questions in the space provided.

1. Explain the difference between short-term, medium-term, and long-term goals for your business. How do your business goals relate to your marketing strategy?

_____

_____

_____

_____

_____

_____

_____

_____

_____

2. Why does a business need a marketing plan?

_____

_____

_____

_____

_____

_____

_____

_____

_____

3. What kinds of information must be included in a marketing plan?

_____

_____

_____

_____

_____

_____

_____

_____

_____

5.2   The Marketing Mix—Product

True or False

Directions   Place a *T* for True or an *F* for False in the Answers column to show whether each of the following statements is true or false.

Answers

1. Over the past 50 years, the U.S. market has changed from being a consumer-driven market to being a product-driven market.

1._____

2. The marketing concept can give small businesses an advantage over larger businesses.

2._____

3. The product mix often includes items of convenience for customers even though those products may not be profitable.

3._____

4. For many businesses, a small percentage of their product mix often makes up the majority of the sales revenue.

4._____

5. Not every product has features.

5._____

6. Product features include such things as color, size, quality, warranties, delivery, and installation.

6._____

7. The brand is the name, symbol, or design used to identify your product.

7._____

8. Products within the same category, such as cars, are positioned in the market to serve different customer needs.

8._____

9. Examining the competition's positioning strategy can help you determine the best positioning strategy for your target market.

9._____

Multiple Choice

Directions   In the Answers column, write the letter that represents the word, or group of words, that correctly completes the statement.

Answers

1. Companies that use the marketing concept will (a) focus on product features more than on consumer needs, (b) select a product mix that will most appeal to their target market, (c) make sure that all products and services they offer are profitable, (d) all of these.

1._____

2. The marketing concept (a) gives large businesses an advantage over small businesses, (b) states that consumers buy a product because it meets their wants or needs, (c) allows large businesses to be more flexible when trying to satisfy customer needs, (d) none of these.

2._____

3. A product mix (a) is the different products and services that a business sells, (b) identifies features such as color, size, and quality, (c) is used to maximize sales, (d) helps determine the pricing strategy.

3._____

4. Product characteristics that will satisfy customer needs are called (a) brands, (b) the product mix, (c) services, (d) features.

4._____

5. The Nike "swoosh" is an example of a product (a) label, (b) brand, (c) feature, (d) package.

5._____

6. When a company offers different products and services within the same category, (a) it is trying to serve different customer needs, (b) its position strategy has failed, (c) it has failed to take the competition into account, (d) it will be unable to make a profit.

6._____

7. Creating an image for a product in the customer's mind is called (a) positioning, (b) branding, (c) packaging, (d) distributing.

7._____

8. To satisfy a specific customer need, a business (a) sets price objectives, (b) uses cost-based pricing, (c) positions its product in a certain market, (d) uses channels of distribution.

8._____

Problem Solving

Directions   Answer the following questions in the space provided.

1. Identify the item at right as a brand, package, or label. Explain your answer.

_____

_____

_____

_____

_____

_____

_____

Nutrition Facts	
Serving Size 1 cup (227g)	
Servings Per Container about 4	

Amount per Serving	
Calories 120	Calories from Fat 20

	% Daily Value*
Total Fat 2g	3%
Saturated Fat 1.5g	8%
Trans Fat 0g	
Cholesterol 10mg	3%
Sodium 150mg	6%
Total Carbohydrate 18g	6%
Dietary Fiber 3g	12%
Sugars 15g	
Protein 10g	

Vitamin A 0%	Vitamin C 0%
Calcium 40%	Iron 0%

*Percent Daily Values are based on a 2,000 calorie diet.

2. Name an automobile model that is positioned to satisfy customers' need for high quality and status. Then name an automobile model that is positioned to satisfy a need for inexpensive transportation. Describe the type of consumer who would buy each of the brands you name. Explain how the automakers of the models you have chosen use product features, branding, and positioning to make their products "stand out" from others and differentiate them in the marketplace.

_____

_____

_____

_____

_____

_____

_____

_____

_____

3. Define the terms *product mix* and *positioning*, and give an example of each for a retail bookstore.

_____

_____

_____

_____

_____

_____

_____

_____

_____

5.3 The Marketing Mix—Price

True or False

Directions Place a *T* for True or an *F* for False in the Answers column to show whether each of the following statements is true or false.

Answers

1. The price is the actual amount that a customer pays for a product or service.

   1. _____

2. The return on investment (ROI) is the amount earned as a result of the investment and is expressed in fractions.

   2. _____

3. To determine the market share of a business, the total market for a product must be known.

   3. _____

4. Your market share rarely depends on the level of competition in your market.

   4. _____

5. Demand-based pricing uses surveys to find out the maximum price that customers would pay for a product.

   5. _____

6. Many businesses mark down items below their cost as a way to make quick profits.

   6. _____

7. With competition-based pricing, the price charged is the same as the price charged by competitors.

   7. _____

8. When services are combined under one charge, rather than making the customer pay for each individual part of the service, this is called price skimming.

   8. _____

9. Price lining involves offering different levels of prices for a specific category of product based on features and quality.

   9. _____

Multiple Choice

Directions In the Answers column, write the letter that represents the word, or group of words, that correctly completes the statement.

Answers

1. Businesses should always set their prices (a) lower than their competitors' prices, (b) based on their product mix, (c) high enough to make a profit, (d) all of these.

   1. _____

2. All of the following are examples of pricing objectives *except* (a) increase profits, (b) minimize sales, (c) attract customers, (d) discourage competition.

   2. _____

3. A company can increase market share through all of the following ways *except* (a) networking, (b) advertising, (c) promotional campaigns, (d) price discounts.

   3. _____

4. A business may set its prices for products or services by using (a) competition-based pricing, (b) cost-based pricing, (c) demand-based pricing, (d) all of these.

   4. _____

5. Cost-based pricing is determined by (a) considering what competitors charge for the same product or service, (b) using the wholesale cost of an item as the basis for the price charged, (c) finding out how much customers are willing to pay for a product or service, (d) analyzing customer need.

   5. _____

6. Which of the following pricing techniques is often used in the introductory stage of a product? (a) Penetration pricing, (b) Prestige pricing, (c) Trade discounts, (d) Markdown pricing.

   6. _____

7. If the terms of an invoice read "2/10, net 30," this means that (a) a 2 percent discount may be taken if the invoice is paid within 30 days, (b) a 2 percent discount may be taken if the invoice is paid within 10 days, (c) one-fifth of the invoice amount must be paid within 30 days, (d) none of these.

   7. _____

8. Which of the following is *not* a discount pricing strategy? (a) Cash discounts, (b) Quality discounts, (c) Seasonal discounts, (d) Trade discounts.

   8. _____

Problem Solving

Directions Answer the following questions in the space provided.

1. What is market share? How is it determined? How can a business increase its market share?

    _____

    _____

    _____

    _____

    _____

    _____

    _____

2. Explain how price is determined using each of the following methods:

    Demand-based pricing

    _____

    _____

    _____

    _____

    Cost-based pricing

    _____

    _____

    _____

    _____

    Competition-based pricing

    _____

    _____

    _____

    _____

3. What is psychological pricing? Identify and describe two strategies used in psychological pricing.

    _____

    _____

    _____

    _____

    _____

    _____

Chapter 5 Assessment
Market Your Business

Vocabulary Review

Directions In the space provided, write a sentence that correctly uses each of the following terms. Your sentence should *not* be a definition of the term.

1. marketing strategy

2. positioning

3. networking

4. return on investment

Fill-in-the-Blank

Directions For each item below, determine the word(s) that best complete the sentence. Write the word(s) in the Answers column.

Answers

1. The four elements of the _____ are product, price, distribution, and promotion.

1. _____

2. The different products and services that a business sells are its _____.

2. _____

3. _____ pricing strategies include price skimming and penetration pricing.

3. _____

4. A(n) _____ is calculated by subtracting a percentage amount from the retail price of an item.

4. _____

5. _____ refers to the costs of making and marketing a product.

5. _____

6. _____ offers customers a reduced price to encourage them to buy.

6. _____

7. Product characteristics that will satisfy customer needs are called _____.

7. _____

8. The _____ is the box, container, or wrapper in which the product is placed.

8. _____

9. A business's market _____ will depend on the level of competition in its market.

9. _____

10. The _____ is the belief that the wants and needs of customers are the most important consideration when developing any product or marketing effort.

10. _____

11. _____ is the process of selling your idea to a company for the development and launch of a new product.

11. _____

12. As part of your _____, you should include performance standards that will help you measure your effectiveness.

12. _____

Problem Solving

Directions   Answer the following questions in the space provided.

1. List six questions that investors will expect your marketing plan to answer.

_____

_____

_____

_____

_____

_____

_____

_____

_____

2. Marcos has invested $7,500 in his submarine sandwich shop near a local college. He wants to earn a 15 percent return on investment (ROI). How much will he need to earn to meet his goal?

_____

_____

_____

_____

3. Midori operates a sunglasses kiosk at a local mall. She buys a certain style of sunglasses for $12.50 a pair. To cover her operating expenses and allow for a profit, she adds 40 percent to her wholesale cost. What is the markup amount on the sunglasses? What is the retail price of the sunglasses?

_____

_____

_____

_____

4. How does a business's product mix help to satisfy customers? Use your answer to explain why a bakery might offer several different varieties of bread.

_____

_____

_____

_____

_____

_____

_____

6.1   The Marketing Mix—Distribution

True or False

Directions   Place a *T* for True or an *F* for False in the Answers column to show whether each of the following statements is true or false.

Answers

1. Channels of distribution are the routes that products take from the time they are produced to the time they arrive at a retail store.

   1. _____

2. No intermediaries are involved in the manufacturer to retailer to consumer channel option.

   2. _____

3. Retail stores can distribute their products to consumers by having convenient hours for customers, shipping directly to consumers, and being accessible through the Internet.

   3. _____

4. Most entrepreneurs who own service businesses sell their services directly to consumers.

   4. _____

5. Service businesses do not have a single, direct channel of distribution if there is more than one store in the chain.

   5. _____

6. A product may move through several channel members by various forms of transportation to get it to the point where it will ultimately be sold to consumers.

   6. _____

7. If you are shipping a large item to another country, you would likely use the U.S. Postal Service.

   7. _____

8. Even businesses that do not sell goods to customers must receive goods from suppliers.

   8. _____

Multiple Choice

Directions   In the Answers column, write the letter that represents the word, or group of words, that correctly completes the statement.

Answers

1. Distribution is an important component of (a) a business's marketing strategy, (b) market research, (c) supply chain management, (d) networking.

   1. _____

2. Intermediaries are used in (a) direct channels of distribution, (b) indirect channels of distribution, (c) the manufacturer-to-consumer channel option, (d) all of these.

   2. _____

3. The most cost-effective channel of distribution option is (a) manufacturer to retailer to consumer, (b) manufacturer to consumer, (c) manufacturer to wholesaler to retailer to consumer, (d) consumer to retailer.

   3. _____

4. In which channel of distribution option does the manufacturer *not* get involved in selling? (a) Manufacturer to consumer, (b) Manufacturer to retailer to consumer, (c) Manufacturer to wholesaler to retailer to consumer, (d) Manufacturer to agent to wholesaler to retailer to consumer.

   4. _____

5. Which of the following service businesses would use a retailer to distribute their services? (a) Electrician, (b) Lawyer, (c) Film developer, (d) Accountant.

   5. _____

6. Manufacturers (a) have a single, direct channel of distribution, (b) distribute their products both broadly and through selected outlets, (c) usually sell directly to consumers, (d) all of these.

   6. _____

7. Which of the following is an example of intellectual property? (a) Inventions, (b) Songs, (c) Artistic designs, (d) All of these.

   7. _____

8. Physical distribution includes all of the following *except* (a) branding, (b) handling of products, (c) transportation, (d) packaging of products.

   8. _____

9. Storing products (a) typically reduces their cost, (b) eliminates the risk that they will be stolen, (c) helps balance supply and demand of products, (d) increases their shelf-life.

   9. _____

Problem Solving

Directions   Answer the following questions in the space provided.

1. What are channels of distribution?

   _____

   _____

   _____

   _____

   _____

2. List three different channels of distribution for a dishwasher manufacturer.

   _____

   _____

   _____

   _____

   _____

3. Where can you find information about distributors, wholesalers, and manufacturers for a retail business?

   _____

   _____

   _____

   _____

   _____

4. Describe some of the benefits gained by both manufacturers and consumers when an intermediary is used in a channel of distribution. Give a real-world example with your answer.

   _____

   _____

   _____

   _____

   _____

   _____

   _____

   _____

   _____

6.2 The Marketing Mix—Promotion

True or False

Directions   Place a *T* for True or an *F* for False in the Answers column to show whether each of the following statements is true or false.

Answers

1. Using an advertising agency is a cost-effective way for a small business to advertise its products or services.

   1._____

2. Online advertising is a more cost-effective way than traditional advertising media for businesses to reach potential customers.

   2._____

3. Television advertising is expensive and generally reaches too broad an audience for most businesses.

   3._____

4. An advantage of radio advertising is that it is relatively inexpensive compared with television or print advertising.

   4._____

5. Newspapers are the best type of advertising media to use when targeting a specific market.

   5._____

6. QR (Quick response) Codes allow magazine advertising to be used in conjunction with online advertising.

   6._____

7. You typically can provide more information on a billboard than you can on a transit ad.

   7._____

8. Although publicity is free, it can be negative if the media coverage is unfavorable.

   8._____

9. Self-promotion is considered a good way to generate "free" publicity.

   9._____

Multiple Choice

Directions   In the Answers column, write the letter that represents the word, or group of words, that correctly completes the statement.

Answers

1. A paid form of communication sent out by a business about a product or service is (a) publicity, (b) sales promotion, (c) advertising, (d) a press release.

   1._____

2. An online ad that displays in a new window that opens in front of the current window is called a (a) pop-up ad, (b) wallpaper ad, (c) banner ad, (d) floating ad.

   2._____

3. Which of the following is *not* a form of online advertising? (a) Email marketing, (b) Rich media ads, (c) Quick response ads, (d) Social media marketing.

   3._____

4. A disadvantage of radio advertising is that (a) it is a purely audio message, (b) ads are required to be submitted weeks or even months in advance, (c) it is very expensive, (d) it reaches too broad an audience to be effective.

   4._____

5. Newspaper advertising is (a) the best type of media for targeting a specific market, (b) relatively expensive compared with television and radio advertising, (c) not effective for mass marketing, (d) the oldest form of advertising in the United States.

   5._____

6. A disadvantage of direct mail advertising is that (a) it has a low response rate, (b) it does not have a high reach, (c) mailing lists for target markets that are available for purchase are expensive, (d) none of these.

   6._____

7. Transit advertising includes ads placed on (a) buildings, (b) taxis, (c) billboards, (d) privately-owned automobiles.

   7._____

8. Publicity (a) is generated by media coverage, (b) may involve staging an event or bringing in a celebrity, (c) may be favorable or unfavorable, (d) all of these.

   8._____

9. The body of a press release should (a) include a few sentences that describes your organization, (b) start on the same line as the dateline, (c) be no more than two paragraphs, (d) all of these.

   9._____

Problem Solving

Directions Complete the following table by naming one advantage and one disadvantage of each of the forms of advertising listed.

Type of Advertising	Advantage	Disadvantage
Online		
Television		
Radio		
Newspaper		
Direct mail		
Magazine		
Outdoor		
Transit		

6.3 Selling and Promoting

True or False

Directions Place a *T* for True or an *F* for False in the Answers column to show whether each of the following statements is true or false.

Answers

1. A salesperson is often the only representative of the company that customers ever come in contact with.

   1._____

2. Personal selling is direct communication between a prospective buyer and a sales representative in which the sales representative attempts to influence the prospective buyer in a purchase situation.

   2._____

3. Benefits are the physical characteristics or capabilities of the product or service.

   3._____

4. Conducting a needs assessment involves interviewing a customer to determine his or her specific needs and wants.

   4._____

5. Satisfying a need is sometimes called problem resolution.

   5._____

6. Emotional buying decisions are based on the desire to have a specific product or service.

   6._____

7. A coupon is a type of rebate.

   7._____

8. A disadvantage of using telemarketing as a promotional strategy is that it is expensive.

   8._____

9. An increased sales conversion rate and a positive return on investment are two ways to measure the effectiveness of promotional activities.

   9._____

Multiple Choice

Directions In the Answers column, write the letter that represents the word, or group of words, that correctly completes the statement.

Answers

1. Selling skills become more important when customers (a) know exactly what they want, (b) try to satisfy their basic needs, (c), are making rational buying decisions, (d) seek to meet their upper-level needs.

   1._____

2. To be successful at selling a product or service, a salesperson must (a) have thorough knowledge of the features and benefits of the product or service, (b) have several years of experience, (c) be able to effectively satisfy customers' lower-level needs, (d) all of these.

   2._____

3. The physical characteristics or capabilities of a product or service are called (a) add-ons, (b) benefits, (c) features, (d) options.

   3._____

4. When customers know exactly what they want, the fulfillment of their needs is referred to as (a) need satisfying, (b) needs assessment, (c) personal selling, (d) rational buying.

   4._____

5. Which of the following is *not* a rational buying motive? (a) Safety, (b) Product quality, (c) Protection (d) Convenience.

   5._____

6. All of the following are emotional buying motives *except* (a) pride of ownership, (b) appearance, (c) simplicity, (d) comfort.

   6._____

7. The first step in the consumer decision-making process is to (a) identify various solutions, (b) define the problem, (c) gather information, (d) evaluate alternatives.

   7._____

8. Contests, free samples, coupons and rebates are examples of (a) telemarketing, (b) sales promotion, (c) publicity, (d) advertising.

   8._____

9. Visual marketing includes the use of (a) logos, (b) uniforms, (c) signage, (d) all of these.

   9._____

Problem Solving

Directions   Answer the following questions in the space provided.

1. In the table below, identify three products that you or your family recently purchased. List some features and benefits of each product.

Product	Features	Benefits

2. You are a salesperson in a mobile phone store. The brand-new Yakker 6800 Mobile Phone has the following features:

- Unique and Innovative Design
- High-Resolution Full-Color Display
- Compact Size
- Camera to Take Snapshots
- Synchronize Data by Linking Directly to Your PC

A customer has entered the store and is interested in the Yakker 6800. In the table below, associate each of the product features with a possible corresponding benefit for this customer.

Features	Benefits
Unique and Innovative Design	
High-Resolution Full-Color Display	
Compact Size	
Camera To Take Snapshots	
Synchronize Data by Linking Directly to Your PC	

Entrepreneurship: Ideas in Action, 6e, Student Edition

Chapter 6 Assessment
Distribution, Promotion, and Selling

Vocabulary Review

Directions   In the Answers column, write the letter that represents the word, or group of words, that correctly completes the statements.

Answers

1. Direct communication between a prospective buyer and a sales representative in which the sales representative attempts to influence the prospective buyer in a purchase decision

2. The routes that products and services take from the time they are produced to the time they are consumed

3. A paid form of communication sent out by a business about a product or service

4. Using the phone to market your product or service

5. The act of establishing a favorable relationship with customers and the general public

6. Purchase decisions that are based on the logical reasoning of customers

7. A nonpaid form of communication that calls attention to your business through media coverage

8. Purchase decisions that are based on the desire to have a specific product or service

9. The coordination of manufacturers, suppliers, and retailers working together to meet a customer need for a product or service

a. advertising
b. channels of distribution
c. emotional buying decisions
d. personal selling
e. public relations
f. publicity
g. rational buying decisions
h. supply chain management
i. telemarketing

1._____

2._____

3._____

4._____

5._____

6._____

7._____

8._____

9._____

Fill-in-the-Blank

Directions   For each item below, determine the word(s) that best complete the sentence. Write the word(s) in the Answers column.

Answers

1. _____ is designed to protect the product from the time it is produced until it is consumed.

2. The strategy created by adopting a blend of advertising, publicity, personal selling, and sales promotion is called your _____.

3. A(n) _____ ad is a kind of online ad in which graphic images or animation are displayed within a rectangular box across the top or down the side of a web page.

4. _____ are digital audio files about various topics that can be downloaded from the Internet.

5. Billboards and signs are examples of _____ advertising.

6. In addition to advertising, publicity, and personal selling, a business can offer sales _____ as a way to increase sales.

7. A(n) _____ is a refund offered to people who purchase a product.

8. Advantages that can result from features are called _____.

9. _____ are people or businesses that move products between the manufacturer and the consumer.

1._____

2._____

3._____

4._____

5._____

6._____

7._____

8._____

9._____

Problem Solving

Directions   Answer the following questions in the space provided.

1. You plan to start a dog-walking service in your community. You have prepared a thorough business plan, identified potential customers, and secured financing for your business. Now you are ready to get the word out to your target market. What kind of promotions will you use to get customers to patronize your new business?

_____

_____

_____

_____

2. How can you determine the best method for transporting goods?

_____

_____

_____

_____

3. Use examples to explain how sales promotions can increase sales.

_____

_____

_____

_____

4. Identify and describe the three most common ways that online advertising is purchased.

_____

_____

_____

_____

_____

_____

_____

_____

_____

_____

_____

Entrepreneurship: Ideas in Action, 6e, Student Edition

7.1 Decide to Purchase, Join, or Start a Business

True or False

Directions Place a *T* for True or an *F* for False in the Answers column to show whether each of the following statements is true or false.

Answers

1. A business broker is a person who sells homes for a living.

1. _____

2. A disadvantage of buying an existing business is that it may be poorly located.

2. _____

3. A valuator can help determine a price to offer for a business and can write a sales contract.

3. _____

4. The owner of a franchise must pay a weekly or monthly royalty fee to the seller of the franchise.

4. _____

5. Advertising fees for franchises are paid directly to the advertisers.

5. _____

6. The Federal Trade Commission regulates franchises.

6. _____

7. The Franchise Disclosure Document helps the franchise buyer to make a knowledgeable purchase.

7. _____

8. An advantage of owning a franchise is that owners have more freedom in making decisions than other entrepreneurs.

8. _____

9. According to some estimates, as many as 90 percent of all businesses are owned by families.

9. _____

Multiple Choice

Directions In the Answers column, write the letter that represents the word, or group of words, that correctly completes the statement.

Answers

1. An advantage of buying an existing business is that (a) there will not be any customer goodwill, (b) suppliers are lined up, (c) it is making a profit, (d) less capital is required.

1. _____

2. When buying an existing business, you should analyze financial accounting reports of operations for at least (a) six months, (b) one year, (c) two years, (d) three years.

2. _____

3. When buying a business, you should do all of the following *except* (a) meet with the business seller, (b) visit during business hours to observe the business in action, (c) inspect a list of all customers, (d) have a lawyer draw up the sales contract.

3. _____

4. If you decide to purchase a franchise, you will have to pay (a) royalty fees, (b) an initial franchise fee, (c) advertising fees, (d) all of these.

4. _____

5. State and federal laws require that the franchisor provide the franchisee with the Franchise Disclosure Document (FDD) (a) at least 14 days before the franchisee signs the contract, (b) when the franchisee signs the contract, (c) at least 30 days before the franchisee signs the contract, (d) when the initial franchise fee is paid.

5. _____

6. The FDD contains all of the following information *except* (a) the name and address of at least 200 current franchisees, (b) a brief history of the franchise, (c) the franchisor's responsibilities to the franchisee, (d) a brief description of every criminal action that the officers have been involved in.

6. _____

7. Franchisors may offer (a) to help finance the purchase, (b) to waive the royalty fees, (c) free nationwide advertising, (d) management and technical training.

7. _____

8. Which of the following is *not* a disadvantage of working in a family business? (a) There is often no exit strategy, (b) Family politics often enter into decision making, (c) The distinction between business life and private life is blurred, (d) A family business may offer less flexibility than other types of businesses.

8. _____

Problem Solving

Directions   Answer the following questions in the space provided.

1. Choose one advantage of buying an existing business and explain why it is an advantage.

   _____

   _____

   _____

   _____

   _____

   _____

2. Choose one disadvantage of buying an existing business and explain why it is a disadvantage.

   _____

   _____

   _____

   _____

   _____

   _____

3. Which costs of purchasing a franchise would you still have if you start your own business?

   _____

   _____

   _____

   _____

4. Which costs of purchasing a franchise would *not* be incurred if you start your own business?

   _____

   _____

   _____

5. The franchise costs in Question 4 pay for benefits that reduce the risk of uncertainty in starting your own business. Explain why.

   _____

   _____

   _____

   _____

   _____

   _____

7.2 Choose a Legal Form of Business

True or False

Directions Place a *T* for True or an *F* for False in the Answers column to show whether each of the following statements is true or false.

Answers

1. Sole proprietorships enable two or more people to be in control of a business.   1._____

2. The government exercises very little control over sole proprietorships.   2._____

3. The most common form of business ownership in the United States is the corporation.   3._____

4. In a partnership, any losses the business incurs will be shared by all of the partners.   4._____

5. A partnership agreement identifies the type and value of the investment contributed by each partner.   5._____

6. People who own shares of stock in a corporation are the owners of the corporation.   6._____

7. A corporation's senior officers decide how much should be paid out in dividends.   7._____

8. A corporation pays taxes both on its income and on the amount it pays out in dividends.   8._____

9. Unlike regular corporations, an S corporation is not taxed as a business.   9._____

Multiple Choice

Directions In the Answers column, write the letter that represents the word, or group of words, that correctly completes the statement.

Answers

1. A business that has the legal rights of a person and may have many owners is a (a) sole proprietorship, (b) partnership, (c) corporation, (d) dual partnership.   1._____

2. A business is a sole proprietorship if it (a) is owned exclusively by one person, (b) has fewer than ten employees, (c) has the legal rights of a person, (d) all of these.   2._____

3. An advantage of a partnership is that (a) the personal assets of partners may not be taken to pay off debts of the partnership, (b) it faces very little government regulation, (c) it is easy to raise capital, (d) it has the legal rights of a person.   3._____

4. Which of the following is *not* included in a partnership agreement? (a) Names of the partners, (b) Conditions under which the partnership can be dissolved, (c) How dividends are to be distributed, (d) Rights of each partner to review accounting documents.   4._____

5. In a corporation, each share of stock is (a) sold by a director of the company, (b) used to determine the amount of income tax, (c) a unit of ownership in the company, (d) a liability.   5._____

6. The board of directors of a corporation (a) is responsible for the day-to-day management of the corporation, (b) determines the salaries of the corporation's officers, (c) pays dividends to shareholders, (d) may be held liable for all company debts.   6._____

7. A disadvantage of a corporation is (a) it is more difficult to set up than a sole proprietorship or a partnership, (b) double taxation, (c) it is subject to heavy government regulation, (d) all of these.   7._____

8. Many companies establish themselves as S corporations (a) because they lose money in their early years, (b) to avoid tedious recordkeeping procedures, (c) to avoid strict government regulation, (d) so that individual shareholders do not have to pay taxes on the profits they earn.   8._____

9. Owners of a limited liability company are known as (a) directors, (b) shareholders, (c) officers, (d) members.   9._____

Problem Solving

Directions   Answer the following questions in the space provided.

1. What are the advantages and disadvantages of a sole proprietorship?

    _____

    _____

    _____

    _____

    _____

2. What are the advantages and disadvantages of a partnership?

    _____

    _____

    _____

    _____

    _____

3. What are the advantages and disadvantages of a corporation?

    _____

    _____

    _____

    _____

    _____

    _____

4. Suppose a company has debts of $120,000 when it goes out of business. Determine the liability in each of the following situations:

    a. The company is a sole proprietorship.

        _____

        _____

    b. The company is a partnership with three partners. The partners have agreed to share profits and losses equally.

        _____

        _____

    c. The company is a corporation with 100 shares of stock worth $1,000 each. There are five shareholders; one owns 60 shares of stock and each of the other four owns 10 shares.

        _____

        _____

7.3 Legal Issues and Business Ownership

True or False

Directions   Place a *T* for True or an *F* for False in the Answers column to show whether each of the following statements is true or false.

Answers

1. The Clayton Act makes it illegal for competitors to get together and set prices on the products or services they sell.

   1. _____

2. The Antitrust Division of the Federal Trade Commission takes legal action against any business it believes has tried to monopolize an industry.

   2. _____

3. The original, creative work of an artist or inventor is called intellectual property.

   3. _____

4. During the period a patent is in effect, no business or individual can copy or use the patented invention without the patent holder's permission.

   4. _____

5. Copyrights remain in effect for 20 years after the death of the author.

   5. _____

6. Regulations that protect consumers include trademarks, zoning regulations, and consumer protection laws.

   6. _____

7. The Consumer Product Safety Act of 1972 sets safety standards for products other than food and drugs.

   7. _____

8. Consideration occurs when one party in a contract offers or agrees to do something and the other party accepts.

   8. _____

Multiple Choice

Directions   In the Answers column, write the letter that represents the word, or group of words, that correctly completes the statement.

Answers

1. Which of the following antitrust legislation laws makes it illegal for competitors to get together and set prices on the products or services they sell? (a) Sherman Act, (b) Clayton Act, (c) Robinson–Patman Act, (d) Wheeler–Lea Act.

   1. _____

2. Which of the following antitrust legislation laws makes it illegal to discriminate by charging different prices to costumers? (a) Sherman Act, (b) Clayton Act, (c) Wheeler–Lea Act, (d) Robinson–Patman Act.

   2. _____

3. The antitrust legislation law that bans false advertising is the (a) Wheeler–Lea Act, (b) Clayton Act, (c) Robinson–Patman Act, (d) Sherman Act.

   3. _____

4. A copyright lasts (a) for 20 years, (b) for the life of the author plus 50 years, (c) for the life of the author plus 70 years, (d) until the author dies.

   4. _____

5. Zoning regulations (a) are enforced by the Federal Trade Commission, (b) control what types of buildings can be built in specific areas, (c) protect consumers from harmful products and unfair business practices, (d) must be approved by the residents of a community.

   5. _____

6. Which of the following laws requires lenders to inform consumers about all costs of credit before an agreement is signed? (a) Sherman Act, (b) Clayton Act, (c) Truth-in-Lending Act, (d) Fair Credit Billing Act.

   6. _____

7. The Federal Trade Commission monitors all of the following activities *except* (a) false or misleading advertising, (b) price setting by competitors, (c) price discrimination, (d) the sale of unhealthful foods.

   7. _____

8. Which of the following is *not* an element of a tort? (a) Injury, (b) Duty, (c) Causation, (d) Capacity.

   8. _____

Problem Solving

Directions   The following table describes various laws that entrepreneurs should know and understand. Complete the table by identifying each law by name.

Description of Law	Name of Law
States that names, symbols, or special marks that distinguish certain businesses can be used only by the business	
Sets safety standards for products other than food and drugs	
States that it is illegal for a business to require a customer to purchase one good in order to be able to purchase another good	
Helps consumers correct credit card billing errors	
Makes it illegal for competitors to get together and set prices on the products or services they sell	
Gives an inventor the sole right to make, use, and sell an invention	
Bans the sale of impure, improperly labeled, falsely guaranteed, and unhealthful foods, drugs, and cosmetics	
Bans unfair or deceptive actions or practices by businesses that may cause an unfair competitive advantage	
Makes it illegal to discriminate by charging different prices to customers	

Entrepreneurship: Ideas in Action, 6e, Student Edition

Chapter 7 Assessment
Select a Type of Ownership

Vocabulary Review

Directions   In the space provided, write a sentence that correctly uses each of the following terms. Your sentence should *not* be a definition of the term.

1. franchise

2. sole proprietorship

3. contract

4. intellectual property

Fill-in-the-Blank

Directions   For each item below, determine the word(s) that best complete the sentence. Write the word(s) in the Answers column.

Answers

1. An advantage to buying an existing business is that it may have built up _____, or customer loyalty.

   1. _____

2. A(n) _____ is a relationship that allows one party to act in a way that legally binds another party.

   2. _____

3. A(n) _____ is a wrong against people or organizations for which the law grants a remedy.

   3. _____

4. A(n) _____ is the person who purchases a franchise agreement.

   4. _____

5. _____ are distributions of corporate profits to the shareholders.

   5. _____

6. _____ means that a corporation's profits are taxed as corporate income and again as individual income.

   6. _____

7. Ownership of a(n) _____ is in the form of shares of stock.

   7. _____

8. A(n) _____ is the grant of a property right to an inventor to exclude others from making, using, or selling his or her invention.

   8. _____

9. _____ are weekly or monthly payments made by the local owner to the franchise company.

   9. _____

10. A(n) _____ is a name, symbol, or special mark used to identify a business.

    10. _____

11. A(n) _____ is an expert on determining the value of a business.

    11. _____

12. A(n) _____ occurs when a company buys a competing firm.

    12. _____

Problem Solving

Directions   Answer the following questions in the space provided.

1. The first column of the following table lists various criteria that entrepreneurs can use to assess business opportunities. Some criteria are based on characteristics of successful entrepreneurs; others are important considerations in business ownership. Rank from 1 to 4 the four types of entrepreneurial opportunities discussed in this chapter. A rank of 1 means the opportunity has the best chance of satisfying the criteria.

	Purchase an existing business	Enter a family business	Purchase a franchise	Start a business
Allows independence				
Encourages creativity				
High personal satisfaction				
Freedom to make decisions				
Low initial cost				
High initial profits				
High profit potential				
Normal working hours				
Low risk				
Easy to run initially				
Easy to acquire or start				
Easy to obtain financing				

2. Describe some conclusions you can draw from the table.

_____

_____

_____

_____

3. Do you think a person's strengths, weaknesses, and aptitudes influence the type of ownership chosen for a business? Explain your answer.

_____

_____

_____

_____

8.1 Choose a Location

True or False

Directions Place a *T* for True or an *F* for False in the Answers column to show whether each of the following statements is true or false.

Answers

1. Neighborhood shopping centers are often called strip malls. — 1._____

2. Community shopping centers are small shopping centers that serve a certain neighborhood. — 2._____

3. Warehouses are generally one of the most expensive rental facilities for a retail business. — 3._____

4. Wholesale companies need a location that attracts a lot of retail traffic. — 4._____

5. Industrial parks are usually located away from housing developments and downtown areas. — 5._____

6. An advantage of working at home is that many costs are reduced or eliminated. — 6._____

7. The cost of maintaining an online business is much less than the cost of buying or leasing a building. — 7._____

8. Your trade area is the area where all of your competitors are located. — 8._____

Multiple Choice

Directions In the Answers column, write the letter that represents the word, or group of words, that correctly completes the statement.

Answers

1. Neighborhood shopping centers (a) are good locations for stores selling goods or services that people need to purchase frequently, (b) typically have low rent, (c) are typically anchored by a supermarket, (d) all of these. — 1._____

2. Many downtown areas have lost business to shopping centers due to (a) lack of convenient parking, (b) higher crime rate, (c) a lack of consumers in the evening, (d) all of these. — 2._____

3. All of the following describe super-regional shopping centers *except* (a) they house more than 100 stores, (b) they charge high rents, (c) they are recommended for new business owners, (d) they are typically anchored by three or more department stores. — 3._____

4. Which of the following is *not* true about businesses operating in warehouses? (a) They are located near other retailers, (b) They have very low rent, (c) They do not have to look appealing on the inside, (d) They must advertise heavily. — 4._____

5. Operating a home-based business (a) offers tax savings, (b) increases networking opportunities, (c) makes business expansion easier, (d) all of these. — 5._____

6. Which of the following is a disadvantage of running a virtual business? (a) Collecting information about customer behavior is difficult, (b) Maintaining a website requires special expertise, (c) Competing with larger, established businesses is difficult, (d) It requires a lot of startup capital. — 6._____

7. A key factor in determining where an industrial business locates is (a) drive-by traffic, (b) availability of good employees, (c) adequate parking, (d) property of nearby businesses. — 7._____

8. When selecting a site for your business, you should do all of the following *except* (a) locate as close as you can to your direct competitors, (b) buy a map and mark your trade area, (c) consider locating near complementary businesses, (d) inspect and evaluate all possible locations. — 8._____

Problem Solving

Directions   Answer the following questions in the space provided.

1. For each of the following businesses, decide what would be an appropriate location. Give reasons for your location selection.

    a. Florist

    _____

    _____

    _____

    _____

    _____

    b. Hardware store

    _____

    _____

    _____

    _____

    _____

    c. Hair salon

    _____

    _____

    _____

    _____

    _____

    d. Office supply store

    _____

    _____

    _____

    _____

    _____

2. Why would a community want to attract industrial businesses by subsidizing rents?

    _____

    _____

    _____

    _____

8.2   Obtain Space and Design the Physical Layout

True or False

Directions   Place a *T* for True or an *F* for False in the Answers column to show whether each of the following statements is true or false.

Answers

1. Most entrepreneurs prefer to lease space for their businesses.

1._____

2. In a gross lease, the landlord pays property taxes and the tenant pays rent, insurance, and any other expenses.

2._____

3. The percentage lease is most common for prime retail locations.

3._____

4. You should always consult an attorney before signing a commercial lease agreement.

4._____

5. Rent per customer equals the amount of rent times the number of projected customers.

5._____

6. A scale drawing of your floor plan will help identify potential problems in your layout.

6._____

7. A retail business should have at least 10 feet of aisle space.

7._____

8. Wholesalers should design a layout that facilitates shipping and receiving.

8._____

9. Attractiveness is the most important design factor for a manufacturing business.

9._____

Multiple Choice

Directions   In the Answers column, write the letter that represents the word, or group of words, that correctly completes the statement.

Answers

1. Most entrepreneurs lease business space because (a) it helps them obtain financing, (b) they prefer to stay in a particular location, (c) they lack the money to purchase property, (d) all of these.

1._____

2. A lease in which the landlord pays all property expenses is a (a) net lease, (b) gross lease, (c) tax-free lease, (d) percentage lease.

2._____

3. A lease in which the landlord receives a percentage of the tenant's revenue each month in addition to rent is a (a) net lease, (b) gross lease, (c) tax-free lease, (d) percentage lease.

3._____

4. A possible location for a business has rent of $975 per month and projected traffic of 9,600 customers per month. Rent per customer is (a) $0.08, (b) $0.10, (c) $0.98, (d) $0.11.

4._____

5. The layout, outside sign, and window displays of your business (a) should match your image, (b) should be similar to other retail businesses in the area, (c) are less important than the name of your business, (d) should never be changed.

5._____

6. The goal of your layout should be to (a) attract customers to your store, (b) meet the needs of your business, (c) gain repeat business, (d) all of these.

6._____

7. In designing a layout for a retail business, you should (a) place the cash register in the back of the store, (b) leave at least 4 feet of aisle space, (c) always use fluorescent lighting, (d) all of these.

7._____

8. The layout of an on-site service business (a) should emphasize organization, (b) is not important, (c) should be similar to a retail business, (d) needs an attractive window display.

8._____

9. All of the following are important for a manufacturing business's layout *except* (a) supervisors should sit near each other, (b) exits should be clearly marked, (c) hazardous materials should be stored safely, (d) work teams should be situated close together.

9._____

Problem Solving

Directions   Answer the following questions in the space provided.

1. Why do most businesses prefer to lease space rather than buy a building?

_____

_____

_____

_____

_____

2. Determine the rent per customer for each of the following. (Round to the nearest cent.)

Location	Rent per month	Projected customer traffic per month	Rent per customer
Downtown	$1,200	9,500	
Community shopping center	$2,800	18,000	
Stand-alone store	$1,050	7,400	

3. What would need to be included in a floor plan for a shop that sells and repairs bicycles and sells bicycle accessories?

_____

_____

_____

_____

_____

4. How can the layout of a wholesale business improve efficiency?

_____

_____

_____

_____

5. Is a floor plan necessary for a home-based business? Why or why not?

_____

_____

_____

_____

8.3 Purchase Equipment, Supplies, and Inventory

True or False

Directions   Place a *T* for True or an *F* for False in the Answers column to show whether each of the following statements is true or false.

Answers

1. Inventory consists of the products that a business sells to its customers and the materials needed to make those products.   1._____

2. A startup business should initially purchase the minimum quantity of equipment and supplies needed.   2._____

3. Vendors are also called suppliers.   3._____

4. You should always choose the vendor who provides the lowest price.   4._____

5. Retail, service, and manufacturing businesses must purchase inventory before they can open for business.   5._____

6. For a manufacturing business, inventory is merchandise purchased with the intent of either reselling it or using it to produce the business's finished product.   6._____

7. A startup business should not tie up too much cash in inventory.   7._____

8. Ongoing businesses usually have a good idea of how much inventory they need to operate.   8._____

Multiple Choice

Directions   In the Answers column, write the letter that represents the word, or group of words, that correctly completes the statement.

Answers

1. Sources of vendor information include all of the following *except* (a) the Internet, (b) insurance agencies, (c) trade magazines, (d) SCORE.   1._____

2. An estimate of how much you will pay for merchandise is (a) a quantity discount, (b) the financing terms, (c) a quote, (d) a letter of intent.   2._____

3. Which of the following types of business does *not* always need inventory before it can open for business? (a) Service, (b) Manufacturing, (c) Retailing, (d) Wholesaling.   3._____

4. For a retail business, inventory consists of (a) merchandise to be resold to customers, (b) parts needed to produce the business's finished product, (c) supplies, (d) all of these.   4._____

5. Determining the amount of inventory to keep in stock is particularly difficult for owners of new businesses because (a) their insurance may not cover damage to stored inventory, (b) they need to take advantage of quantity discounts, (c) they do not know what their level of sales will be, (d) all of these.   5._____

6. To make sure you do not run out of stock unexpectedly, you can (a) establish a reorder point for each product that you sell, (b) store extra inventory at a warehouse, (c) use only suppliers who guarantee to deliver in one day, (d) all of these.   6._____

7. A reorder point (a) is an order to a supplier for additional items, (b) is a predetermined level of inventory that signals when new stock must be purchased, (c) should only be set for products that have high sales, (d) none of these.   7._____

8. How low you set your reorder point depends on all of the following *except* (a) how many units of the item you sell each month, (b) how long it takes your supplier to get the merchandise to you, (c) how important it is to you not to be out of stock, (d) the number of customers you have each month.   8._____

Problem Solving

Directions Answer the following questions in the space provided.

1. The first column of the following table lists the types of standard equipment and supply needs for most businesses. Complete the table by listing three items for each type of need.

Type	Items
Furniture	
Fixtures	
Office equipment	
Office supplies	
Maintenance supplies	
Kitchen supplies	

2. Describe the different types of inventory.

_____

_____

_____

_____

_____

_____

3. For each type of inventory, what are the consequences of being out of stock of a particular item?

_____

_____

_____

_____

_____

4. How can a business manage its inventory so it does not run out of stock unexpectedly?

_____

_____

_____

_____

_____

Entrepreneurship: Ideas in Action, 6e, Student Edition

Chapter 8 Assessment
Locate and Set Up Your Business

Vocabulary Review

Directions   For each definition given, write the term defined in the appropriate squares.

1. A type of lease in which a tenant pays a base rent, and the landlord also receives a percentage of the tenant's revenue each month

⬜⬜⬜⬜⬜⬜⬜⬜⬜⬜⬜⬜ ⬜⬜⬜⬜⬜⬜

2. The geographic area from which you expect to attract a majority of your customers

⬜⬜⬜⬜⬜⬜ ⬜⬜⬜⬜⬜⬜

3. The products that a business sells to its customers as well as the materials needed to make those products

⬜⬜⬜⬜⬜⬜⬜⬜⬜⬜⬜

4. A section of land that is zoned for industrial business only

⬜⬜⬜⬜⬜⬜⬜⬜⬜⬜⬜ ⬜⬜⬜⬜⬜

5. The person who owns and rents out buildings or space

⬜⬜⬜⬜⬜⬜⬜⬜⬜

Fill-in-the-Blank

Directions   For each item below, determine the word(s) that best complete the sentence. Write the word(s) in the Answers column.

Answers

1. Other businesses in a shopping center benefit from the advertising done by _____ stores.

1. _____

2. Because they are of basic construction with few frills inside or out, _____ are generally one of the cheapest rental facilities.

2. _____

3. _____ shopping centers usually have 40 to 100 stores, a retail area of 400,000 to 800,000 square feet, and are anchored by two or more large department stores.

3. _____

4. A(n) _____ lease occurs when the landlord pays building insurance, and the tenant pays rent, property taxes, and any other expenses.

4. _____

5. In a(n) _____ lease, the tenant pays rent each month for the space occupied, and the landlord covers all property expenses for that space.

5. _____

6. You will need to prepare a(n) _____ drawing of the layout of your business.

6. _____

7. _____ consists of buying and selling products or services over the Internet.

7. _____

8. To fill the standard and special equipment and supply needs of your business, you will have to research suppliers, or _____.

8. _____

9. Before you purchase merchandise for your business, you should get a(n) _____, or estimate, of how much you will have to pay.

9. _____

10. The _____ is a predetermined level of inventory that signals when new stock should be ordered.

10. _____

Problem Solving

Directions   Lee Torres plans to open a retail pet store. The store will carry high-quality dog and cat foods; leashes, collars, and coats for dogs; scratching posts and trees for cats; and carriers, beds, toys, treats, grooming needs, and flea products for both dogs and cats. Lee does not plan to sell puppies or kittens but will have a large assortment of birds, tropical fish, and small animals (hamsters, guinea pigs, and so on) and the foods and accessories needed for them. The store will also carry an assortment of books about the selection, training, and care of pets. Answer the following questions in the spaces provided.

1. If Lee's store will be in a large metropolitan area, what would be a good location for the business? Why?

    _____

    _____

    _____

2. If Lee's store will be in a small city or town, what would be a good location for the business? Why?

    _____

    _____

    _____

    _____

    _____

3. What are some general considerations for the layout of the pet store?

    _____

    _____

    _____

    _____

4. In the box below, design a layout of the store.

9.1 Financing Your Business

True or False

Directions Place a *T* for True or an *F* for False in the Answers column to show whether each of the following statements is true or false.

Answers

1. Net worth is the difference between items of value that you own and amounts you owe to others.

    1. _____

2. To calculate your net worth, you should prepare a pro forma financial statement.

    2. _____

3. Your company's debt-to-equity ratio measures how much money a company can safely borrow over time.

    3. _____

4. Equity capital does not include money invested by the owner of the business.

    4. _____

5. Venture capitalists are usually interested in companies that have the potential of earning hundreds of millions of dollars within a few years.

    5. _____

6. Debt capital is money invested in a business in return for a share in the profits of the business.

    6. _____

7. A bank usually will loan a business up to 50 percent of the total value of its accounts receivable if it feels that that business's customers are good credit risks.

    7. _____

8. Banks require collateral for most unsecured loans.

    8. _____

9. The Small Business Administration (SBA) does not make direct loans.

    9. _____

Multiple Choice

Directions In the Answers column, write the letter that represents the word, or group of words, that correctly completes the statement.

Answers

1. Before you can approach a lender or investor about financing your business, you must prepare all of the following *except* (a) a personal cash flow statement, (b) a personal financial statement, (c) a pro forma balance sheet, (d) a pro forma income statement.

    1. _____

2. Items of value that you own are called (a) liabilities, (b) net worth, (c) equity, (d) assets.

    2. _____

3. A high debt-to-equity ratio (a) indicates that a business is primarily financed through equity, (b) indicates that a company may not be able to generate enough cash to meet its debt obligations, (c) is usually preferred by lenders, (d) none of these.

    3. _____

4. Venture capitalists are individuals or companies that (a) make a living by investing in startup companies, (b) have few criteria for lending money, (c) are sponsored by the SBA, (d) help small businesses find investors.

    4. _____

5. Unsecured loans are (a) backed by collateral, (b) usually interest free, (c) usually short-term loans that have to be repaid within a year, (d) easier to get than secured loans.

    5. _____

6. A line of credit (a) is a type of secured loan, (b) has a fee whether or not money is actually borrowed, (c) is a type of debt capital, (d) all of these.

    6. _____

7. If a business wants to make improvements to increase profits, it will usually get a (a) line of credit, (b) long-term loan, (c) startup loan, (d) short-term loan.

    7. _____

8. A bank may turn down a loan application for a new business because the entrepreneur (a) is too confident, (b) has previously owned a business, (c) is investing too little of his or her own money in the business, (d) none of these.

    8. _____

9. Although similar to borrowing from the SBA, the restrictions are tighter for borrowing from (a) the Department of Housing and Urban Development, (b) state governments, (c) the Economic Development Association, (d) Small Business Investment Companies.

    9. _____

Problem Solving

Directions   Answer the following questions in the space provided.

1. Explain the difference between equity capital and debt capital.

    _____

    _____

    _____

    _____

    _____

2. List five sources of equity capital.

    _____

    _____

    _____

    _____

    _____

3. List five sources of debt capital.

    _____

    _____

    _____

    _____

    _____

4. Do you think it is better for an entrepreneur to finance a business with equity capital or debt capital? Explain your answer.

    _____

    _____

    _____

    _____

    _____

5. Describe a secured loan and an unsecured loan, and list four kinds of secured loans.

    _____

    _____

    _____

    _____

    _____

9.2 Pro Forma Financial Statements

True or False

Directions Place a *T* for True or an *F* for False in the Answers column to show whether each of the following statements is true or false.

Answers

1. A cash flow statement shows a business's revenues and expenses incurred over a period of time and the resulting profit or loss.

1._____

2. A best-case-scenario cash flow statement should project the lowest cash receipts and highest cash disbursements that your business is likely to have.

2._____

3. An income statement is sometimes called a profit/loss statement.

3._____

4. An income statement shows revenues that you have received and expenses that you have paid.

4._____

5. Interest earned from bank accounts is considered revenue.

5._____

6. The cost of the inventory that a business sells during a particular period is called cost of goods sold.

6._____

7. A business that has more assets than liabilities has negative net worth.

7._____

8. Inventory is a type of fixed asset because it is used up in normal business operations.

8._____

9. Loans and accounts payable are examples of liabilities.

9._____

Multiple Choice

Directions In the Answers column, write the letter that represents the word, or group of words, that correctly completes the statement.

Answers

1. If cash receipts total more than cash disbursements, your business has (a) a negative cash flow, (b) a positive cash flow, (c) positive net worth, (d) negative net worth.

1._____

2. An income statement indicates (a) actual cash coming in and going out of a business, (b) how much money a business earns or loses over a period of time, (c) expenses that you have not yet received, (d) your total current assets.

2._____

3. An income statement helps you do all of the following *except* (a) identify categories of expenditures you may want to decrease, (b) examine how sales are changing over time, (c) forecast how well your business can expect to perform in the future, (d) anticipate when negative cash flows will occur so that you can plan for how to handle them.

3._____

4. The difference between revenue and cost of goods sold is called (a) gross profit, (b) owner's equity, (c) net cash flow, (d) none of these.

4._____

5. The assets, liabilities, and owner's equity of a business are shown on a(n) (a) income statement, (b) profit/loss statement, (c) balance sheet, (d) cash flow statement.

5._____

6. In the accounting equation, assets must always equal (a) liabilities plus owner's equity, (b) liabilities minus owner's equity, (c) owner's equity minus liabilities, (d) current liabilities plus long-term liabilities.

6._____

7. On a balance sheet, buildings and furniture would be included as (a) long-term liabilities, (b) fixed assets, (c) current assets, (d) accounts receivable.

7._____

8. A mortgage is a type of (a) current liability, (b) account payable, (c) long-term liability, (d) fixed asset.

8._____

9. Depreciation is included on a balance sheet to show that some (a) accounts are uncollectible, (b) assets have been sold, (c) assets have lost value over time, (d) expenses have not been paid.

9._____

Problem Solving

Directions   Answer the following questions in the space provided.

1. The following table lists items that appear on various financial statements. Complete the table by identifying the financial statement on which the item should appear.

Item	Financial Statement
Utilities expenses due	
Cash received for goods sold	
Accounts payable	
Depreciation	
Rent paid	
Forecasted revenues	
Uncollectible accounts	
Insurance paid	

2. Many of the items included on a list of startup costs also appear on a balance sheet. Why?

_____

_____

_____

_____

_____

_____

3. Explain the difference between accounts receivable and accounts payable.

_____

_____

_____

_____

_____

_____

4. Write the accounting equation, and define each element in it.

_____

_____

_____

_____

_____

9.3 Recordkeeping for Businesses

True or False

Directions   Place a *T* for True or an *F* for False in the Answers column to show whether each of the following statements is true or false.

Answers

1. Under the cash method of accounting, revenue is recorded prior to receipt.

   1. _____

2. The cash flow statement is prepared using the accrual method of accounting.

   2. _____

3. Typically, only very small businesses use the cash method of accounting.

   3. _____

4. If you receive supplies today but pay for them later, you should record this transaction in the cash payments journal.

   4. _____

5. Subsidiary ledgers are commonly used for accounts payable and accounts receivable.

   5. _____

6. An aging table is a recordkeeping tool for tracking accounts payable.

   6. _____

7. Payroll records show employee earnings and any deductions from those earnings.

   7. _____

8. Deductions from employee's earnings include federal, state, and local taxes and contributions for Social Security and Medicare.

   8. _____

9. A business that collects sales tax must pay the tax quarterly.

   9. _____

Multiple Choice

Directions   In the Answers column, write the letter that represents the word, or group of words, that correctly completes the statement.

Answers

1. The accrual method of accounting (a) is used by most companies because it offers a better picture of long-term profitability, (b) does not report expenses that have been incurred but not yet paid, (c) must be used by businesses with sales of more than $10 million a year, (d) is more difficult and tedious to use than the cash method.

   1. _____

2. A sales journal is used to record only (a) purchases of merchandise on account, (b) sales of merchandise on account, (c) cash payment transactions, (d) cash receipt transactions.

   2. _____

3. The journal used to record any kind of transaction is the (a) sales journal, (b) cash payments journal, (c) general journal, (d) ledger journal.

   3. _____

4. Which of the following is *not* one of the journals that businesses typically use to record their transactions? (a) General journal, (b) Cash receipts journal, (c) Expense journal, (d) Sales journal.

   4. _____

5. Posting is generally done (a) on a weekly basis, (b) every one to two days, (c) whenever a transaction occurs, (d) when a business receives its monthly bank statement.

   5. _____

6. An aging table shows a business (a) the status of their inventory, (b) how long it is taking customers to pay their bills, (c) how long it is taking suppliers to ship products, (d) cash sales and cash payments received from customers on their credit accounts.

   6. _____

7. A booklet in which you record the dates and amounts of the checks you have written is called a(n) (a) aging account, (b) subsidiary ledger, (c) check register, (d) payroll register.

   7. _____

8. A payroll register includes all of the following information *except* (a) an employee's regular and overtime earnings, (b) federal taxes deducted from an employee's earnings, (c) sales taxes deducted from an employee's earnings, (d) an employee's Social Security contribution.

   8. _____

9. A business must pay income taxes (a) at the end of each month, (b) even when it does not earn a profit, (c) twice a year, (d) quarterly.

   9. _____

Problem Solving

Directions   Answer the following questions in the space provided.

1. Name and describe the five different journals that businesses use to record their transactions.

_____

_____

_____

_____

_____

_____

_____

_____

_____

_____

_____

_____

_____

_____

_____

_____

_____

2. For each of the following business activities, identify all the places where the activity should be recorded.

Business Activity	Journal	Ledger	Other
Purchase of merchandise on account			
Payment of utilities bill			
Cash sale			
Weekly deposit of cash and checks			
Sale of merchandise on account			
Payment of employee wages			

Chapter 9 Assessment
Plan and Track Your Finances

Vocabulary Review

Directions   In each of the following sentences, the underlined term is not used correctly, In the space provided, rewrite the sentence so the term is used correctly.

1. <u>Liabilities</u> are items of value owned by a business, such as cash, equipment, and inventory.

2. A <u>transaction</u> is any business activity that changes revenues or expenses and should be reconciled from the general ledger to the journal.

3. For an unsecured loan, a bank requires <u>collateral</u>, such as real estate or an insurance policy.

Fill-in-the-Blank

Directions   For each item below, determine the word(s) that best complete the sentence. Write the word(s) in the Answers column.

Answers

1. Financial statements based on projections are known as _____ financial statements.

    1. _____

2. _____ are amounts owed to vendors for merchandise purchased on credit.

    2. _____

3. The assets, liabilities, and owner's equity of a business at a particular point in time are shown on a(n) _____.

    3. _____

4. _____ is money invested in a business in return for a share in the profits of the business.

    4. _____

5. A(n) _____ loan is usually made for a very specific purpose and must be repaid within a year.

    5. _____

6. A(n) _____ is an accounting record that provides financial detail for a particular business item.

    6. _____

7. The difference between _____ and cost of goods sold is the gross profit.

    7. _____

8. A(n) _____ is a recordkeeping tool for tracking accounts receivable.

    8. _____

9. Any cash, check, or electronic payment that a business makes is recorded in the _____ journal.

    9. _____

10. A(n) _____ is a list of people who receive salary or wage payments from a business.

    10. _____

11. _____ is the use of the Internet to fund a business venture or project by raising money from a large number of people.

    11. _____

12. Current assets are often referred to as _____ because they can be converted to cash easily.

    12. _____

Problem Solving

Directions Answer the following questions in the space provided.

1. Name and describe three kinds of tax records that a business must keep.

    _____

    _____

    _____

    _____

    _____

    _____

    _____

    _____

    _____

    _____

2. A retail pet store has $10,500 in cash and inventory worth $31,250. The store has a six-year bank loan of
    $40,000 and current liabilities of $360. The office equipment for the store is worth $10,500, less $1,150 in
    depreciation; store fixtures are worth $8,700, less $600 in depreciation; and a company vehicle is worth
    $10,500, less $1,500 in depreciation. Accounts receivable are $1,050 and accounts payable are $9,800.

    a. What are the store's current assets, fixed assets, and total assets? (Show your work.)

        _____

        _____

        _____

        _____

        _____

    b. What are the store's current liabilities, long-term liabilities, and total liabilities? (Show your work.)

        _____

        _____

        _____

        _____

    c. What is the owner's equity? (Show your work.)

        _____

        _____

        _____

        _____

10.1   Operating Procedures

True or False

Directions   Place a *T* for True or an *F* for False in the Answers column to show whether each of the following statements is true or false.

Answers

1. All functions of management work together and are continuous.

   1. _____

2. Planning is the process of establishing operating procedures that make effective use of people and other resources.

   2. _____

3. Organizational structure is a plan that shows how the various jobs in a company relate to one another.

   3. _____

4. The authoritative management style is often used in a crisis situation when there is not enough time to let the group participate in the decision-making process.

   4. _____

5. Combining democratic and participatory management styles is called mixed management.

   5. _____

6. An effective manager understands that all employees prefer to be involved in day-to-day decision making.

   6. _____

7. As part of the control function, you will routinely review your plans and make adjustments.

   7. _____

8. Rules are more specific than procedures.

   8. _____

9. A business must have a hiring policy.

   9. _____

Multiple Choice

Directions   In the Answers column, write the letter that represents the word, or group of words, that correctly completes the statement.

Answers

1. Rules, policies, and procedures, are important components of (a) strategic planning, (b) intermediate-range planning, (c) short-term planning, (d) none of these.

   1. _____

2. All of the following are included in the organizing function *except* (a) assigning tasks, (b) hiring employees, (c) grouping tasks into departments, (d) allocating resources.

   2. _____

3. Training and compensating the employees of a business is part of which of the following management functions? (a) Staffing, (b) Planning, (c) Implementing, (d) Controlling.

   3. _____

4. The management style *most* appropriate to use with a new group of employees who do not have previous experience in the type of work being performed is (a) mixed management, (b) participatory management, (c) democratic management, (d) authoritative management.

   4. _____

5. If standards are not being met, a manager may need to (a) hire new employees, (b) upgrade to higher-quality production materials, (c) change operating procedures, (d) all of these.

   5. _____

6. "Employees may smoke only in designated smoking areas" is an example of a company (a) rule, (b) procedure, (c) directive, (d) policy.

   6. _____

7. Policies (a) outline the appropriate behavior of those that work for you, (b) are instructions on how to perform a task correctly, (c) may apply to both employees and customers, (d) should be adhered to in all situations.

   7. _____

8. A policy for replacements, refunds, or repairs (a) is usually not necessary for most businesses, (b) will help maintain customer goodwill, (c) negatively impacts profits, (d) none of these.

   8. _____

Problem Solving

Directions   Answer the following questions in the space provided.

1. Name and describe the five functions of management.

    _____

    _____

    _____

    _____

    _____

    _____

    _____

    _____

    _____

    _____

    _____

    _____

2. The table below lists five tasks often performed by managers. Name which one of the five functions of management is represented by each task.

Task	Management Function
Deciding which job you will assign to which employee	
Hiring a new employee	
Completing the monthly budget	
Conducting a yearly performance appraisal for an employee	
Writing a memo to an employee instructing her how to accomplish a task	

3. Zhang Wei operates a Chinese restaurant and is thinking about offering delivery services for carryout orders. What kinds of things must he plan before offering a delivery service?

    _____

    _____

    _____

    _____

    _____

10.2 Inventory Control

True or False

Directions Place a *T* for True or an *F* for False in the Answers column to show whether each of the following statements is true or false.

Answers

1. Direct costs of inventory include storage, insurance, and taxes.

1. _____

2. The most important aspect of inventory management is having items in stock when they are needed.

2. _____

3. The perpetual inventory method is commonly used by small businesses with limited inventories.

3. _____

4. Businesses that sell more than 50 different items usually track inventory electronically.

4. _____

5. Point-of-sale software updates inventory records as each sale happens.

5. _____

6. The amount of inventory recorded when taking a physical count will always be the same as the amount listed in a perpetual inventory system.

6. _____

7. Establishing reorder points is a way to avoid stockouts.

7. _____

8. The stock turnover rate shows how many times a year a business sells all of its merchandise.

8. _____

9. To calculate the stock turnover rate, divide inventory by sales.

9. _____

Multiple Choice

Directions In the Answers column, write the letter that represents the word, or group of words, that correctly completes the statement.

Answers

1. Inventory control involves (a) establishing reorder points, (b) determining when you need the most inventory in stock, (c) scheduling deliveries to arrive at the point in time when you need the items, (d) all of these.

1. _____

2. The amount of inventory you need to purchase can be calculated from the (a) sales forecast, (b) balance sheet, (c) cash flow statement, (d) income statement.

2. _____

3. All of the following should be recorded on an inventory record *except* (a) the item's cost, (b) the item's stock number, (c) the amount of inventory you currently have, (d) the maximum amount you want in inventory at any time.

3. _____

4. A company that uses the perpetual inventory method should take a physical count of inventory (a) daily, (b) weekly, (c) monthly, (d) yearly.

4. _____

5. A low stock report shows (a) that a physical count of inventory should be taken, (b) the number of units of each item to order, (c) the number of units sold, (d) when items should be ordered.

5. _____

6. The level of inventory you keep in stock depends on (a) the stock turnover rate, (b) the costs of carrying inventory, (c) the cost of lost sales due to being out of stock, (d) all of these.

6. _____

7. The costs of holding inventory are (a) deteriorating costs, (b) fixed costs, (c) carrying costs, (d) stock turnover costs.

7. _____

8. If a hardware store maintains an inventory of 20 for a particular snow shovel and sells 60 of these snow shovels in a year, the stock turnover rate for that snow shovel is (a) 0.33, (b) 3, (c) 60, (d) 1,200.

8. _____

9. If the stock turnover rate for your industry is 3, how many months' worth of inventory should you keep in stock at all times? (a) 2, (b) 3, (c) 4, (d) 9.

9. _____

Problem Solving

Directions   Answer the following questions in the space provided.

1. How does the type of business help to determine the method used for tracking inventory?

_____

_____

_____

_____

_____

_____

_____

2. How does the product or service of a business help to determine the method used for tracking inventory?

_____

_____

_____

_____

_____

3. What other factors might influence a business's choice of inventory tracking method?

_____

_____

_____

_____

_____

4. Explain how carrying costs, out-of-stock costs, and the stock turnover rate each contributes to determining the level of inventory that a business should keep in stock.

_____

_____

_____

_____

_____

_____

10.3 Financial Management

True or False

Directions Place a *T* for True or an *F* for False in the Answers column to show whether each of the following statements is true or false.

Answers

1. A cash budget should be based on actual past revenues and operating expenses. 1._____

2. To encourage customers who owe you money to pay more quickly, you can offer discounts on bills paid immediately. 2._____

3. Reducing your payroll expenses by laying off workers can improve your cash flow. 3._____

4. You can reduce fixed expenses to improve your cash flow. 4._____

5. The three most important elements of a company's financial strength are its cash inflows, cash outflows, and net income. 5._____

6. Net profit on sales is calculated by dividing net income after taxes by net sales. 6._____

7. Net sales is the dollar amount of all sales, including sales that have been returned. 7._____

8. The breakeven point is the volume of sales that must be made to cover all of the expenses of a business. 8._____

9. The more debt a business has, the more risk it is taking. 9._____

10. For good financial health, a company's debt ratio should be 1 or more. 10._____

Multiple Choice

Directions In the Answers column, write the letter that represents the word, or group of words, that correctly completes the statement.

Answers

1. Offering discounts on bills paid right away will (a) increase your cash receipts, (b) get customers to pay more quickly, (c) decrease your accounts receivable, (d) all of these. 1._____

2. You can increase cash receipts by (a) establishing tighter credit policies, (b) holding shipments to customers with large unpaid bills, (c) establishing a follow-up system for collecting unpaid accounts receivable, (d) all of these. 2._____

3. You can decrease your cash disbursements by (a) holding more inventory, (b) paying your bills more promptly, (c) increasing the size of your workforce, (d) none of these. 3._____

4. Analyzing your sales by product can help you (a) determine the amount of income tax to pay, (b) find the breakeven point, (c) make decisions about the kind of inventory to stock, (d) determine whether or not your business is earning a profit. 4._____

5. All of the information necessary for calculating net profit on sales is found on the (a) cash flow statement, (b) balance sheet, (c) income statement, (d) inventory record. 5._____

6. To determine net income after taxes, you must calculate all of the following *except* (a) net income before taxes, (b) gross profit, (c) net sales from operations, (d) net income from operations. 6._____

7. Which of the following must be subtracted from net sales to find gross profit? (a) Cost of goods sold, (b) Operating expenses, (c) Total expenses, (d) Interest expense. 7._____

8. If a company has current assets of $114,270, current liabilities of $47,923, net income totaling $32,170, and total debt of $101,226, what is the company's current ratio? (a) 0.42, (b) 0.67, (c) 2.38, (d) 3.15. 8._____

9. Which of the following ratios is used to measure a company's liquidity (a) current ratio, (b) return on assets, (c) return on equity, (d) debt ratio. 9._____

Problem Solving

Directions Answer the following questions in the space provided.

1. Complete the following income statement.

Revenue from sales	
Gross sales	$183,000
Returns	$1,900
Net sales	
Cost of goods sold	$74,400
Gross profit	
Operating expenses	
Salaries	$32,400
Rent	$12,000
Utilities	$900
Advertising	$1,200
Insurance	$1,200
Other	$780
Total operating expenses	
Net income from operations	
Interest expense	$3,600
Net income before taxes	
Taxes	$13,350
Net income after taxes	

2. Use the income statement from Question 1 to compute net profit on sales. (Show your work.)

_____

_____

_____

3. A pet store owner analyzes sales by department in order to determine whether inventory should be increased or reduced. Determine the total sales, find the percent of sales for each department, and record your answers in the table that follows.

Department	Sales	Percent of Total Sales
Birds	$45,900	
Small animals	$25,800	
Tropical fish	$39,800	
Cats	$81,200	
Dogs	$78,300	
Total		

Entrepreneurship: Ideas in Action, 6e, Student Edition

Chapter 10 Assessment
Operations Management

Vocabulary Review

Directions   In each of the following sentences, the underlined term is not used correctly, In the space provided, rewrite the sentence so the term is used correctly.

1. An <u>organizational structure</u> is a plan that shows the salaries of all company employees.

2. <u>Net income after operations</u> is calculated by subtracting cost of goods sold from net sales.

3. The <u>periodic inventory method</u> keeps track of inventory levels on a daily basis.

Fill-in-the-Blank

Directions   For each item below, determine the word(s) that best complete the sentence. Write the word(s) in the Answers column.

Answers

1. A(n) _____ should show the projections of your cash coming in and going out.

    1. _____

2. The _____ indicates how profitable a company is relative to the total amount of assets invested in the company.

    2. _____

3. _____ is the stock of goods that a business has for sale.

    3. _____

4. Setting broad, long-range objectives to achieve the long-term goals of your business is called _____ planning.

    4. _____

5. A business that has enough money to pay off any debt owed is described as being _____.

    5. _____

6. To calculate your net profit on sales, you need to know your net income after taxes and your _____.

    6. _____

7. At the _____, your sales will equal all of your expenses.

    7. _____

8. _____ is the process of setting standards for the operation of a business and ensuring those standards are met.

    8. _____

9. _____ outline the appropriate behavior and actions of those who work for you.

    9. _____

10. _____ is the process of achieving goals by establishing operating procedures that make effective use of people and other resources.

    10. _____

11. _____ involves directing and leading people to accomplish the goals of the organization.

    11. _____

12. The _____ contains most of the data needed for analyzing a company's debt and equity.

    12. _____

13. A(n) _____ is a paper inventory record for a single item.

    13. _____

Problem Solving

Directions Answer the following questions in the space provided.

1. You own and manage a small retail toy store. You have two employees, who have worked with you for more than 10 years. Because business has been good, you have recently added two new employees, neither of whom has any prior sales experience. What management style will you use with your staff? Explain.

_____

_____

_____

_____

_____

2. Complete the following cash budget.

	A	B	C	D
		Estimated	**Actual**	**Difference**
1	**Cash receipts**			
2	Cash sales	$4,600	$5,900	
3	Accounts receivable payments	$8,280	$9,350	
4	**Total cash receipts**			
5	**Cash disbursements**			
6	Salaries	$3,500	$6,200	
7	Gasoline	$2,700	$3,100	
8	Rent	$1,000	$1,000	
9	Utilities	$75	$83	
10	Advertising	$200	$175	
11	Supplies	$40	$64	
12	Insurance	$100	$100	
13	Other	$65	$82	
14	**Total cash disbursements**			
15	**Net cash increase/decrease**			

3. What does the cash budget show about the company's cash flow? How can the cash flow be improved?

_____

_____

_____

_____

_____

11.1 Identify Your Staffing Needs

True or False

Directions Place a *T* for True or an *F* for False in the Answers column to show whether each of the following statements is true or false.

Answers

1. The people who work for your business are your human resources.

    1._____

2. A job description is the process of determining the tasks and sequence of tasks necessary to perform a job.

    2._____

3. An organizational structure is a plan that shows how the various jobs in a company relate to each other.

    3._____

4. The owner of a large company with many employees should not have to deal with relatively unimportant issues.

    4._____

5. Employment agencies typically charge businesses and/or the job seekers a fee when they are successful in making a match.

    5._____

6. College and university career centers are a good resource for employment opportunities for anyone who is qualified.

    6._____

7. Statistics show that employment sites and classified ads garner the highest number of qualified hires.

    7._____

8. A freelancer is similar to an employee in that the business must pay benefits to the freelancer while he or she is employed by the company.

    8._____

9. Temporary workers include seasonal employees and substitutes for employees who are sick or on a leave of absence.

    9._____

Multiple Choice

Directions In the Answers column, write the letter that represents the word, or group of words, that correctly completes the statement.

Answers

1. To find out your staffing needs, you should ask yourself all of the following questions *except* (a) What skills do I need occasionally? (b) What skills do I have? (c) What skills am I missing? (d) What kinds of employees do I need?

    1._____

2. An organizational chart can help the owner of a company (a) analyze staffing needs, (b) recruit employees, (c) obtain referrals, (d) all of these.

    2._____

3. Who reports to whom in a company is called the (a) line of succession, (b) chain of command, (c) career pathway, (d) ladder of success.

    3._____

4. Which of the following is becoming an increasingly popular way to recruit employees? (a) Social networking sites, (b) Career fairs, (c) Using headhunters, (d) All of these.

    4._____

5. An employment specialist who seeks out highly qualified professionals to fill positions is called a(n) (a) human resources manager, (b) entrepreneur, (c) headhunter, (d) job counselor.

    5._____

6. A want ad should do all of the following *except* (a) briefly describe the position, (b) ask applicants to identify their race and religion, (c) identify any special job requirements, (d) provide instructions on how to apply for the position.

    6._____

7. Which of the following recruiting methods has been shown to garner the highest number of most qualified hires? (a) Employment agencies, (b) Classified ads, (c) Referrals, (d) Classified ads.

    7._____

8. Students who work for little or no pay in order to gain experience in a particular field are (a) freelancers, (b) interns, (c) trainees, (d) available through employment agencies.

    8._____

Problem Solving

Directions   Answer the following questions in the space provided.

1.   In the table below, identify six resources that an employer can use to recruit employees. For each, list one advantage and one disadvantage.

Resource	Advantage	Disadvantage

2.   Describe some advantages of working as a freelancer. What are some possible disadvantages?

_____

_____

_____

_____

_____

_____

_____

_____

_____

_____

Name _____ Class _____ Date _____

11.2 Staff Your Business

True or False

Directions   Place a *T* for True or an *F* for False in the Answers column to show whether each of the following statements is true or false.

Answers

1. The first step of the hiring process is to review and verify information on job applications.

1._____

2. When contacting past employers listed on a job application, you should ask about a candidate's personal qualities.

2._____

3. Indications that a person may not be a good worker include frequent job changes, unexplained gaps in employment, and critical comments about previous employers.

3._____

4. In the job interview, it is okay to make a snap judgment when you know immediately that the candidate is not right for the job.

4._____

5. An employee can receive a bonus regardless of whether he or she is paid a wage or a salary.

5._____

6. A combination plan includes a base salary plus benefits.

6._____

7. Employers are required to provide at least five days of sick leave per year.

7._____

8. The purpose of the Age Discrimination in Employment Act of 1967 is to promote employment of persons age 60 and over based on their ability rather than their age.

8._____

Multiple Choice

Directions   In the Answers column, write the letter that represents the word, or group of words, that correctly completes the statement.

Answers

1. When selling your business during an interview, you should (a) describe your bonus system, (b) talk about the significance of working in a new business, (c) share your values and plans for the business, (d) all of these.

1._____

2. During a job interview, you should (a) check references, (b) use the job description to prepare questions, (c) allow the applicant plenty of time to speak, (d) offer the job if you are impressed with the applicant.

2._____

3. In most markets, wages and salaries are (a) determined by large companies, (b) paid biweekly, (c) determined by the government, (d) competitively determined.

3._____

4. Rewards, other than cash, given to employees are called (a) bonuses, (b) raises, (c) benefits, (d) commissions.

4._____

5. The Affordable Care Act requires businesses with 50 or more full-time equivalent employees to (a) provide at least five days of sick leave, (b) offer competitive wages, (c) provide health insurance, (d) offer some type of retirement plan.

5._____

6. The contract negotiation process between the employer and the union is known as (a) collective bargaining, (b) arbitration, (c) mediation, (d) profit sharing.

6._____

7. The Fair Labor Standards Act of 1938 (a) established the maximum number of hours employees can work, (b) guarantees workers the right to join a union, (c) requires employers to verify that employees are American citizens, (d) prohibits hiring discrimination on the basis of race.

7._____

8. The Family and Medical Leave Act of 1993 requires businesses with more than 50 employees to provide up to 12 weeks unpaid leave if an employee has (a) given birth, (b) a serious health condition, (c) adopted a child, (d) all of these.

8._____

Problem Solving

Directions   Answer the following questions in the space provided.

1. What is the difference between wages and a salary?

    _____

    _____

    _____

    _____

    _____

    _____

2. Describe the advantages to the employee and to the employer for each type of pay listed in the following table.

Type of Pay	Advantages for Employee	Advantages for Employer
Wage		
Salary		
Commission-only salary		
Base salary plus commission		
Bonus		

Entrepreneurship: Ideas in Action, 6e, Student Edition

11.3 Direct and Control Human Resources

True or False

Directions   Place a *T* for True or an *F* for False in the Answers column to show whether each of the following statements is true or false.

Answers

1. Supervisory-level managers have the highest level of responsibility in a company.
    1. _____

2. First-line managers are responsible for implementing the goals of top management.
    2. _____

3. An employee who does not follow established policies concerning vacations, holidays, and hours should be dismissed immediately.
    3. _____

4. Coaching is a training technique in which one employee teams up with a more experienced employee to learn a job.
    4. _____

5. One way to motivate employees is to delegate responsibility.
    5. _____

6. If a company is to grow, the owner must delegate workloads and responsibilities.
    6. _____

7. The implementing function of management involves setting standards for the operation of a business and ensuring those standards are met.
    7. _____

8. A performance evaluation is part of the implementing function of management.
    8. _____

9. Performance reviews should be conducted face to face.
    9. _____

Multiple Choice

Directions   In the Answers column, write the letter that represents the word, or group of words, that correctly completes the statement.

Answers

1. Which managers work directly with the employees on the job? (a) Supervisory-level managers, (b) Middle managers, (c) Administrative-level managers, (d) All of these.
    1. _____

2. Administrative-level managers are responsible for all of the following *except* (a) controlling and overseeing the entire company, (b) developing goals and company policies, (c) guiding and supervising employees, (d) establishing the vision for the company.
    2. _____

3. Employee training should (a) begin as soon as the employee is hired, (b) be evaluated to ensure it was effective, (c) be continuous, (d) all of these.
    3. _____

4. Employees learn about new techniques and trends from an expert in the field (a) during on-the-job training, (b) in coaching sessions, (c) at conferences and seminars, (d) called a mentor.
    4. _____

5. With which of the following training techniques do employees receive feedback and instruction from their manager on a constant basis? (a) Coaching, (b) On-the-job training, (c) Mentoring, (d) Shadowing.
    5. _____

6. All of the following are ways to motivate your employees *except* (a) pay them well, (b) give them less responsibility, (c) treat them fairly, (d) offer public recognition for good work.
    6. _____

7. You should evaluate employee performance (a) once a month, (b) on a job analysis form, (c) to help you identify both outstanding and problem employees, (d) none of these.
    7. _____

8. Promotion decisions should be (a) made fairly, (b) based on employee competition, (c) made at a team meeting, (d) made using the formal decision-making process.
    8. _____

Problem Solving

Directions   Answer the following questions in the space provided.

1. Why might the owner of a manufacturing company establish a company policy requiring all employees to wear protective eye and ear gear?

_____

_____

_____

_____

_____

2. How does a business owner benefit from delegating responsibility?

_____

_____

_____

_____

_____

3. How does a business owner benefit from listening to employees?

_____

_____

_____

_____

_____

4. How does an employer benefit from a yearly evaluation of an employee?

_____

_____

_____

_____

_____

5. How does an employee benefit from a yearly evaluation by an employer?

_____

_____

_____

_____

_____

Entrepreneurship: Ideas in Action, 6e, Student Edition

Chapter 11 Assessment
Human Resource Management

Vocabulary Review

Directions   For each definition given, write the term defined in the appropriate squares.

1. Payments for labor or services that are made on an hourly, daily, or per-unit basis

    ☐☐☐☐☐☐

2. To look for people to hire and attract them to the business

    ☐☐☐☐☐☐☐☐

3. An amount paid for a job position stated on an annual basis

    ☐☐☐☐☐☐☐☐

4. A written statement listing the tasks and responsibilities of a position

    ☐☐☐ ☐☐☐☐☐☐☐☐☐☐☐

5. Serves as a management control tool that helps determine whether the objectives for a particular job are being met

    ☐☐☐☐☐☐☐☐☐☐☐   ☐☐☐☐☐☐☐☐☐☐☐

Fill-in-the-Blank

Directions   For each item below, determine the word(s) that best complete the sentence. Write the word(s) in the Answers column.

Answers

1. A(n) _____ is an organization that represents employees and bargains on their behalf for better working conditions and terms of employment.

    1._____

2. A(n) _____ is a collection of tasks and duties that an employee is responsible for completing.

    2._____

3. _____ are people who provide specialty services to a number of different businesses on an hourly basis or by the job.

    3._____

4. _____ is a compensation arrangement in which employees are paid a portion of the company's profits.

    4._____

5. A financial reward made in addition to a regular wage or salary is a(n) _____.

    5._____

6. A(n) _____ is a percentage of a sale paid to a salesperson.

    6._____

7. A classified advertisement that an employer places in the newspaper to attract job applicants is called a(n) _____.

    7._____

8. To _____ is to let others share workloads and responsibilities.

    8._____

9. _____ are characteristics of a person that cannot be targeted for discrimination.

    9._____

10. A(n) _____ is the process of determining the tasks and sequence of tasks necessary to perform a job.

    10._____

Problem Solving

Directions   Answer the following questions in the spaces provided.

1. Which two steps in the hiring process do you think are most important? Give reasons for your answers.

    _____

    _____

    _____

    _____

    _____

    _____

    _____

2. Which leadership quality do you think is most important? Why?

    _____

    _____

    _____

    _____

    _____

    _____

    _____

3. Which way of motivating employees do you think is most effective? Why?

    _____

    _____

    _____

    _____

    _____

    _____

    _____

4. How can an employer use the yearly performance evaluation as motivation?

    _____

    _____

    _____

    _____

    _____

    _____

    _____

12.1 Business Risks

True or False

Directions   Place a *T* for True or an *F* for False in the Answers column to show whether each of the following statements is true or false.

Answers

1. Natural risks are caused by acts of nature.
   1. _____

2. Political stability is an example of an economic risk that an entrepreneur faces.
   2. _____

3. If you practice risk management, you are assuring your business will never face a loss.
   3. _____

4. To prepare for risks, your first step should be to develop a plan.
   4. _____

5. A recovery plan is an important part of every risk management plan.
   5. _____

6. It is impossible for an entrepreneur to protect his or her business against the different kinds of theft.
   6. _____

7. Electronic devices and security guards are the only steps you can take to prevent or reduce shoplifting.
   7. _____

8. Almost all businesses are vulnerable to robberies.
   8. _____

9. To minimize losses from bad checks, you can establish a policy of accepting checks drawn on in-state banks only.
   9. _____

Multiple Choice

Directions   In the Answers column, write the letter that represents the word, or group of words, that correctly completes the statement.

Answers

1. Human risks (a) are caused by the actions of individuals, (b) are caused by acts of nature, (c) occur because of changes in business conditions, (d) none of these.
   1. _____

2. Looking at all aspects of your business and determining the risks you face is called (a) a recovery plan, (b) risk assumption, (c) risk management, (d) risk assessment.
   2. _____

3. You transfer risk and protect yourself against the financial losses from some risks by (a) installing deadbolt locks, (b) installing an alarm system, (c) installing surveillance systems, (d) purchasing insurance.
   3. _____

4. The National Safety Council recommends that an emergency action plan include all of the following *except* (a) a detailed floor plan of the business, (b) chain-of-command information, (c) facility evacuation procedures, (d) the preferred method for reporting fires.
   4. _____

5. Installing electronic merchandise tags can help to (a) keep track of inventory, (b) increase sales, (c) reduce the risk of shoplifting, (d) all of these.
   5. _____

6. Employee theft (a) cannot be prevented, (b) can negatively impact your business financially, (c) is often undetectable, (d) all of these.
   6. _____

7. With regards to employee theft, you should be on the lookout for (a) employees who work odd hours, (b) vehicles parked close to loading areas, (c) employees who have unexplained close relationships with a customer, (d) all of these.
   7. _____

8. To limit losses in the event of a robbery, a business can (a) install deadbolt locks, (b) hire a security guard, (c) keep a minimal amount of cash in the cash register and transfer any money that exceeds this amount to a safe, (d) encourage credit card use.
   8. _____

9. An electronic credit authorizer (a) allows a business owner to collect credit card fees, (b) checks to see if a credit card is valid, (c) identifies bad checks, (d) allows businesses to accept credit card payments from all major credit card companies.
   9. _____

Problem Solving

Directions   Answer the following questions in the space provided.

1. In the first column of the following table, list the methods that can prevent or reduce shoplifting. Then, rank the methods from 1 to 5 according to effectiveness, cost, and ease of implementation. A ranking of 1 should indicate the most effective, the least expensive, and the easiest to implement.

Method	Effectiveness	Cost	Ease of Implementation

2. In the first column of the following table, list the methods that can prevent or reduce employee theft. Then, rank the methods from 1 to 4 according to effectiveness, cost, and ease of implementation. A ranking of 1 should indicate the most effective, the least expensive, and the easiest to implement.

Method	Effectiveness	Cost	Ease of Implementation

12.2 Insure Against Risks

True or False

Directions   Place a *T* for True or an *F* for False in the Answers column to show whether each of the following statements is true or false.

Answers

1. A pure risk presents the chance of loss but no opportunity for gain.

    1._____

2. Investing in the stock market is an example of a speculative risk.

    2._____

3. All risks are insurable.

    3._____

4. Business interruption insurance covers the loss of income resulting from a fire or other catastrophe that disrupts the operation of the business.

    4._____

5. Liability insurance covers claims of negligent actions by business professionals such as doctors.

    5._____

6. A business owner may buy life insurance so that his or her heirs have enough money to continue the business.

    6._____

7. The financial strength of an insurance company indicates the company's ability to meet its obligations to policyholders.

    7._____

8. The first step in buying insurance is determining how much coverage you need.

    8._____

9. You should always take your insurance agent's word about how much coverage your business needs.

    9._____

Multiple Choice

Directions   In the Answers column, write the letter that represents the word, or group of words, that correctly completes the statement.

Answers

1. The classifications of risk are based on all of the following *except* the (a) result of the risk, (b) timing of the risk, (c) controllability of the risk, (d) insurability of the risk.

    1._____

2. Which of the following types of risk offers you the chance to gain as well as lose from the event or activity? (a) Speculative, (b) Pure, (c) Controllable, (d) Uncontrollable.

    2._____

3. If there is a risk that a loss will occur and the amount of the loss cannot be predicted, the risk is (a) uncontrollable, (b) speculative, (c) uninsurable, (d) all of these.

    3._____

4. Uninsurable risks are tied to all of the following *except* (a) economic conditions, (b) technology changes, (c) competitors' actions, (d) robberies.

    4._____

5. A business faces risk due to (a) an increase in local taxes, (b) poor management, (c) a decline in consumer demand, (d) all of these.

    5._____

6. Many small and mid-sized business purchase a package known as a business owner's policy, which include all of the following *except* (a) property insurance, (b) business interruption insurance, (c) health insurance, (d) liability insurance.

    6._____

7. Which of the following types of insurance covers your company's legal responsibility for the harm it may cause to others as a result of what you and your employees do or fail to do in your business operations? (a) Life insurance, (b) Liability insurance, (c) Property insurance, (d) Business interruption insurance.

    7._____

8. To protect your business against employee theft, you should purchase (a) property insurance, (b) crime insurance, (c) liability insurance, (d) theft insurance.

    8._____

9. The first step in buying insurance is to (a) determine the kinds of coverage you think you need, (b) choose an insurance agent, (c) determine the amounts of coverage you need, (d) identify the kinds of risks you would like to insure against.

    9._____

Problem Solving

Directions   Answer the following questions in the space provided.

1. The first column of the following table lists business risks. Complete the table by identifying the type of insurance that covers each risk.

Risk	Type of Insurance
Death of an owner	
Lawsuit due to an accident on the premises	
Earthquake	
Robbery	
Lawsuit claiming that a defect in a product manufactured or sold caused bodily injury	
Contents owned by the renter inside a leased space are damaged	
Fire	
Flood	
Storm damage	
Extra expense of operating out of a temporary location after a fire has destroyed the building	

2. Describe how to choose an insurance agent.

_____

_____

_____

_____

_____

_____

3. Describe the process for determining insurance coverage for a business.

_____

_____

_____

_____

_____

12.3 Other Risks

True or False

Directions   Place a *T* for True or an *F* for False in the Answers column to show whether each of the following statements is true or false.

Answers

1. When one business allows another business to buy now and pay later, it is offering fair credit.

1. _____

2. Consumer credit is offered in two basic forms: loans and trade credit.

2. _____

3. Collection difficulties are one reason a business chooses to accept credit cards that are issued by banks or credit card companies.

3. _____

4. Most credit cards are considered secured loans.

4. _____

5. Most employers are required by law to provide workers' compensation insurance.

5. _____

6. All injuries suffered on the job are covered by workers' compensation insurance.

6. _____

7. It is the employee's, not the employer's, responsibility to file a workers' compensation claim.

7. _____

8. Exchange rates are dependent on countries' political and economic stability.

8. _____

Multiple Choice

Directions   In the Answers column, write the letter that represents the word, or group of words, that correctly completes the statement.

Answers

1. When one business allows another business to buy now and pay later, it is offering (a) trade credit, (b) consumer credit, (c) an installment loan, (d) secured credit.

1. _____

2. An unsecured loan is (a) granted based on the credit history of the individual, (b) a type of installment loan, (c) backed by collateral, (d) all of these.

2. _____

3. Some things to consider in determining whether or not an applicant is creditworthy include all of the following *except* (a) previous credit history, (b) marital status, (c) employment record, (d) assets owned.

3. _____

4. Uncollectible accounts (a) will not be a problem for a business that has established sound credit policies, (b) are an expense to a business, (c) increase net income, (d) occur only with secured loans.

4. _____

5. All of the following are considered some of the most dangerous occupations in America *except* (a) farmers and ranchers, (b) garbage collectors, (c) construction workers, (d) nurses.

5. _____

6. Which of the following injuries are *not* covered by workers' compensation insurance? (a) Injuries individuals afflict on themselves, (b) Injuries suffered during a fight that the injured employee starts, (c) Injuries suffered while violating employer policies, (d) All of these.

6. _____

7. To minimize the risks of international business, you should (a) conduct business in only one foreign country, (b) never partner with a company that is located in the country you are targeting, (c) learn about the other country's culture, (d) all of these.

7. _____

8. An advantage of hiring a local manager when doing business globally is that the local manager (a) can assist with labor issues, (b) will be able to assist you in any product modifications or changes in business practices you need to make to work with the foreign market, (c) will have a better understanding of the cultural and political scene of the country, (d) all of these.

8. _____

Problem Solving

Directions   Answer the following questions in the space provided.

1. Why would a business decide to accept credit cards issued by banks and credit card companies instead of issuing its own credit card?

_____

_____

_____

_____

_____

_____

2. Describe four challenges that a business may face if it decides to do business in a foreign country.

_____

_____

_____

_____

_____

_____

_____

_____

_____

_____

_____

3. Describe four strategies that a business might take to deal with the risks of conducting business internationally.

_____

_____

_____

_____

_____

_____

_____

_____

_____

_____

_____

Entrepreneurship: Ideas in Action, 6e, Student Edition

Chapter 12 Assessment
Risk Management

Vocabulary Review

Directions   In each of the following sentences, the underlined term is not used correctly, In the space provided, rewrite the sentence so the term is used correctly.

1. A risk is an <u>insurable risk</u> if it is a controllable risk faced by a small number of people and the amount of the loss is substantial.

2. Businesses lose millions of dollars every year because of <u>shoplifting</u>, the act of purchasing goods using a stolen credit card.

3. A <u>bounced check</u> is a check that the business returns to the bank because the payer's savings account has insufficient funds to cover the check amount.

Fill-in-the-Blank

Directions   For each item below, determine the word(s) that best complete the sentence. Write the word(s) in the Answers column.

Answers

1. _____ is the possibility of some kind of loss.   1._____

2. A(n) _____ plan will enable you to get back to business as quickly as possible.   2._____

3. Examples of _____ risks include storms, fires, earthquakes, and floods.   3._____

4. A(n) _____ risk is one that can be reduced or possibly even avoided by actions you take.   4._____

5. A(n) _____ is a payment made to an insurance company to cover the cost of insurance.   5._____

6. To minimize losses from bad checks, a business may establish a policy of accepting checks drawn on _____ banks only.   6._____

7. When a retail business allows its customers to buy merchandise now and pay for it later, it is offering _____.   7._____

8. Most businesses offering credit cards to consumers have them complete a credit application to determine whether they are _____.   8._____

9. Insurance agents earn _____ on the amount of coverage they sell.   9._____

10. _____ injuries result from performing the same activity repeatedly for long periods of time.   10._____

11. A(n) _____ loan is paid back with interest in equal monthly amounts over a specified period of time.   11._____

Problem Solving

Directions   Answer the following questions in the space provided.

1. Explain why some risks are uninsurable.

_____

_____

_____

_____

_____

_____

_____

_____

2. You plan to open a bookstore with a small cafe. List the types of risk you will face. Categorize them as human, natural, or economic, and classify them as controllable/uncontrollable and insurable/uninsurable. For all insurable risks, list the type of insurance that you could purchase to protect against the risk.

_____

_____

_____

_____

_____

_____

_____

_____

_____

3. Suppose you plan to operate a comic book shop near a university. Will you offer customers credit? If not, explain your reasoning. If so, tell what kind of consumer credit you will offer, and develop a credit policy.

_____

_____

_____

_____

_____

_____

_____

_____

13.1 Growth Strategies

True or False

Directions Place a *T* for True or an *F* for False in the Answers column to show whether each of the following statements is true or false.

Answers

1. If the condition of your business shows that you should expand, you should next analyze the economic climate that controls the business.

1. _____

2. Market development is a strategy for expanding the target market of a business.

2. _____

3. A vertical growth strategy involves adding new products and services that complement the company's current product line.

3. _____

4. Growing rapidly is always a good thing for businesses.

4. _____

5. A product goes through five stages in its life cycle.

5. _____

6. During the maturity stage of the product life cycle, both sales and profits decline.

6. _____

7. Once an idea for a new product has been determined to be reasonable, the next step for the business is to create a prototype of the product and test-market it.

7. _____

8. Introduction of the product into the target market is the last step of the product life cycle.

8. _____

Multiple Choice

Directions   In the Answers column, write the letter that represents the word, or group of words, that correctly completes the statement.

Answers

1. Determining when to expand depends on (a) the location of your business, (b) the condition of your business, (c) your product or service, (d) your fixed costs.

1. _____

2. To analyze the economic climate that controls your business, you need to (a) determine whether or not demand for your product or service will remain strong, (b) your competitors' plan to expand, (c) determine whether or not you can obtain financing, (d) all of these.

2. _____

3. Which of the following involves increasing market share for a product or service within a given market in a given area? (a) Geographic expansion, (b) Market penetration, (c) Market development, (d) Product development.

3. _____

4. You can increase your market share by (a) offering special deals to customers, (b) buying new equipment, (c) adding managers to your staff, (d) reducing your variable costs.

4. _____

5. Your plan for expansion should include strategies for (a) assessing the economic condition of your industry, (b) increasing your advertising, (c) hiring managers and supervisors, (d) locating your direct competition.

5. _____

6. In which stage of the product life cycle do sales peak and profits begin to decline? (a) Introduction, (b) Growth, (c) Maturity, (d) Decline.

6. _____

7. The first, and most often difficult, step in new product development is (a) idea development, (b) idea screening, (c) financial analysis, (d) product marketing.

7. _____

8. Which of the following is *not* a question that should be asked during the strategy development stage of product development? (a) Would current customers benefit from the product? (b) Can a quality product be produced at a reasonable cost? (c) What is the likely demand for the product? (d) Would the product enhance the image of the company's overall product mix?

8. _____

Problem Solving

Directions   Answer the following questions in the space provided.

1. The condition of a business and economic conditions indicate to the business owner that the business can expand. The business owner develops strategies for growth and writes an expansion plan. Why might the business owner decide at this point not to expand?

_____

_____

_____

_____

_____

2. Why is it necessary for a business owner to prepare a plan before his or her business?

_____

_____

_____

_____

_____

3. Briefly describe three different growth strategies.

_____

_____

_____

_____

_____

_____

_____

4. List and describe stages in the product life cycle.

_____

_____

_____

_____

_____

_____

_____

_____

_____

13.2 Ethical and Social Issues

True or False

Directions   Place a *T* for True or an *F* for False in the Answers column to show whether each of the following statements is true or false.

Answers

1. Ethics involves choosing between right and wrong.

   1._____

2. Even within the same culture, individuals develop different codes of ethics.

   2._____

3. Due to strict codes of ethics, businesses rarely face ethical dilemmas.

   3._____

4. Employees will not act ethically unless they see the business owner acting in an ethical manner.

   4._____

5. You should create a code of ethics as soon as you begin your business.

   5._____

6. One of your responsibilities to customers is to avoid exaggerating the merits of your products and services.

   6._____

7. Entrepreneurs are legally required to inform customers of possible dangers of the products they sell.

   7._____

8. To make sure you maintain good relationships with suppliers, you should do what they suggest.

   8._____

9. Business owners can contribute to their community by donating money and goods or services.

   9._____

10. An entrepreneur has an obligation to do as little harm as possible to the environment.

    10._____

Multiple Choice

Directions   In the Answers column, write the letter that represents the word, or group of words, that correctly completes the statement.

Answers

1. Ethics is the study of (a) honesty, (b) different cultures, (c) moral choices and values, (d) business behavior.

   1._____

2. Paying bribes is an accepted business practice (a) in some cultures, (b) in all countries, (c) in some parts of the United States, (d) except where prohibited by law.

   2._____

3. All of the following are characteristics of individuals who have a strong work ethic *except* (a) dedication, (b) cooperation, (c) intelligence, (d) productivity.

   3._____

4. Your employees are more likely to act ethically if (a) your business requires a license, (b) they see you acting in an ethical manner, (c) they are well paid, (d) all of these.

   4._____

5. To write an effective code of ethics for your business, you should (a) take a course in ethics, (b) ask a lawyer for guidelines to follow, (c) think about ethical dilemmas that may arise and come up with solutions for dealing with them, (d) all of these.

   5._____

6. If you change suppliers, you should (a) let your current supplier know the reason, (b) give the current supplier time to find another customer to account for the lost sales, (c) inform your customers, (d) inform your creditors and investors.

   6._____

7. A business owner should never conceal risks he or she is facing from (a) customers, (b) competitors, (c) investors, (d) all of these.

   7._____

8. Federal laws concerning clean air and water are enforced by the (a) Environmental Protection Department, (b) Federal Trade Commission, (c) Environmental Protection Agency, (d) Consumer Product Safety Commission.

   8._____

9. Environmental law covers all of the following *except* (a) resource conservation, (b) resource management, (c) pollution control, (d) land-use regulation.

   9._____

Problem Solving

Directions Answer the following questions in the space provided.

1. Explain how culture affects ethical behavior.

   _____

   _____

   _____

   _____

   _____

2. Do consumers sometimes demand higher codes of ethics from businesses than from themselves? Explain your answer.

   _____

   _____

   _____

   _____

   _____

3. What will happen to a business that does not meet its responsibilities to its customers?

   _____

   _____

   _____

   _____

   _____

4. What will happen to a business that does not meet its responsibilities to its suppliers?

   _____

   _____

   _____

   _____

   _____

5. What will happen to a business that does not meet its responsibilities to its community?

   _____

   _____

   _____

   _____

   _____

13.3 Global Trends and Opportunities

True or False

Directions   Place a *T* for True or an *F* for False in the Answers column to show whether
each of the following statements is true or false.

Answers

1. To export their products or services, businesses may hire salespeople or use
    commissioned agents to find foreign buyers.

    1. _____

2. Entrepreneurs may decide to import parts to sell or to use in the production of their
    product.

    2. _____

3. In analyzing the international market, you will have to consider political, economic,
    social, and cultural issues.

    3. _____

4. An international business plan is an extension of your original business plan.

    4. _____

5. Trade protections are established by governments to keep foreign businesses from
    competing with domestic producers.

    5. _____

6. A qualitative restriction is a standard of quality an exported product must meet before it
    can be sent to another country.

    6. _____

7. The North American Free Trade Agreement removed most barriers to trade and
    investment between Mexico, Canada, and the United States.

    7. _____

8. The Office of International Trade, International Trade Administration, and Bureau of
    Industry and Security are agencies of the U.S. Department of Commerce.

    8. _____

Multiple Choice

Directions   In the Answers column, write the letter that represents the word, or group of
words, that correctly completes the statement.

Answers

1. Exporting goods by finding foreign buyers or distributors and then shipping your
    product to them (a) is indirect exporting, (b) requires using commissioned agents, (c) is
    direct exporting, (d) is a benefit of global competition.

    1. _____

2. Exporting through commissioned agents is (a) direct exporting, (b) indirect exporting,
    (c) not recommended for small businesses, (d) not cost-effective.

    2. _____

3. Which of the following is *not* one of the benefits of competing globally? (a) Decreased
    dependence on current markets and suppliers, (b) Reduced costs, (c) Increased sales,
    (d) Less competition.

    3. _____

4. Before you trade internationally, you should write an international business plan that
    indicates (a) when you plan to begin exporting products, (b) what costs you expect to
    have, (c) how you will learn about the culture, (d) who your competitors will be.

    4. _____

5. To help U.S. businesses operate in foreign markets, the federal government offers
    programs in (a) export counseling, (b) export financing, (c) technical assistance, (d) all
    of these.

    5. _____

6. A limit on the amount of a product that can be imported into a country over a particular
    period of time is a (a) quota, (b) markup, (c) tariff, (d) qualitative restriction.

    6. _____

7. A tax on imports is a (a) quota, (b) markup, (c) tariff, (d) qualitative restriction.

    7. _____

8. The Office of International Trade (a) works to improve the global business environment
    and helps U.S. organizations compete and abroad, (b) is an agency of the U.S.
    Department of Commerce, (c) is the Small Business Administration's office for the
    support of small business international trade development, (d) works to ensure an
    effective export control and treaty compliance system.

    8. _____

Entrepreneurship: Ideas in Action, 6e, Student Edition

Problem Solving

Directions   Answer the following questions in the space provided.

1. A business may get involved in international trade via direct exporting, indirect exporting, or the World Wide Web. Which exporting method do you think is easiest? Which is the riskiest? Which requires the most knowledge about a foreign country? Explain your responses.

_____
_____
_____
_____
_____
_____
_____
_____
_____
_____
_____
_____

2. As an exporter, which type of trade barrier do you think would be easiest to deal with?

_____
_____
_____
_____
_____
_____
_____
_____

3. All trade barriers protect domestic producers. Why would a government choose one trade barrier over another?

_____
_____
_____
_____
_____
_____
_____
_____

Chapter 13 Assessment
Management for the Future

Vocabulary Review

Directions   In the Answers column, write the letter that represents the word, or group of words, that correctly completes the statements.

Answers

1. Increasing the market share for a product or service within a given market in a given area

   a. business ethics
   b. code of ethics

   1. _____

2. The application of the principles of right and wrong to issues that come up in the workplace

   c. exports
   d. imports

   2. _____

3. The stages that a product goes through from the time it is introduced to when it is no longer sold

   e. market penetration
   f. product life cycle

   3. _____

4. A standard of quality that an imported product must meet before it can be sold

   g. qualitative restriction

   4. _____

5. A limit on the amount of a product that can be imported into a country over a particular period of time

   h. quota
   i. trade barriers

   5. _____

6. A set of standards or rules that outlines the ethical behavior demanded by an individual, a business, or a culture

   6. _____

7. Products and services that are brought from another country to be sold

   7. _____

8. Products and services that are produced in one country and sent to another country to be sold

   8. _____

9. Methods for keeping foreign businesses from competing with domestic producers

   9. _____

Fill-in-the-Blank

Directions   For each item below, determine the word(s) that best complete the sentence. Write the word(s) in the Answers column.

Answers

1. A tariff is a tax on _____.

   1. _____

2. Ethics is the study of moral choices and _____.

   2. _____

3. A company that expands into new operations to decrease its dependence on other firms in the supply chain is pursuing a(n) _____ growth strategy.

   3. _____

4. In the _____ stage of the product life cycle, a product will attract more customers and sales begin to increase.

   4. _____

5. Businesses should conserve _____ resources, such as coal and oil, by using them efficiently.

   5. _____

6. A(n) _____ is a full-scale model of a new product.

   6. _____

7. Some businesses use commissioned agents who act as _____ to find foreign buyers for products and services.

   7. _____

8. _____ is defined as "ensuring that information is accessible only to those authorized to have access."

   8. _____

9. For _____ exporting, a business may need to hire salespeople who live in or travel to the foreign countries.

   9. _____

Problem Solving

Directions   Answer the following questions in the space provided.

1. In the table below, identify the four stages of the product life cycle and name a currently available product that fits into each stage.

Life Cycle Stage	Product Example

2. Business owners have a responsibility to contribute to their communities. Provide an example of a business in your area that has contributed to the community in some way.

_____

_____

_____

_____

_____

_____

_____

3. Should a business code of ethics be different from a personal code of ethics? Explain your answer.

_____

_____

_____

_____

_____

_____

_____

4. How does it benefit a business to respect the environment?

_____

_____

_____

_____

_____

_____

_____